T0293756

Praise for *Begin With You*

'Navigate the tangled web of mental health and its relationship to modern work life.' VERNON BAINTON, CHIEF MEDICAL OFFICER, HAVAS LYNX GROUP

'Petra Velzeboer brings through a reality and pragmatism when it comes to finding your wellness in this busy, chaotic world we live and work in. Written from the heart and spoken with care.' KIRSTIN FURBER, DIRECTOR OF PEOPLE, CHANNEL 4

'Brings inspiration, practical thinking and true thought leadership that I would recommend to anyone who wants a new angle on how to view their well-being at work.' STELLA SMITH, CEO AND FOUNDER, PIRKX

'Offers empowering practices for claiming ourselves, our well-being and our communities. I felt energized and hopeful reading this book. You will too.' DR ARDESHIR MEHRAN, PSYCHOLOGIST AND AUTHOR

'This book guides the reader through an exploration of how our personal and professional lives are interconnected, allowing us to embrace the idea of focusing on ourselves in order to achieve success at work.' MIRIAM ZYLBERGLAIT LISIGURSKI, MD, FACP

'Petra Velzeboer is in a class of her own! Her passion is centred on helping others and her approach comes from a place of lived experience – an experience that she shares so transparently and unabashedly. This is all reflected in the book and what makes it such a solid, authentic source.' RONDETTE AMOY SMITH, HEAD OF DIVERSITY AND INCLUSION, NOMURA EMEA

'A must-read for virtually anyone, whether you want to build a mental health strategy, are an entrepreneur or business owner or are just interested in practical steps to improve your own mental health. Petra Velzeboer's approach can benefit us all.' HANNAH MEREDITH, HEALTH AND WELL-BEING PARTNER, MVF GLOBAL

'We know a lot about investing in our success, but do we know and talk enough about investing in our mental health? Are we even listening? Petra Velzeboer leads the way and shines a light through the maze of tools and set constructs defined by employers and medical professionals. This book is lively, passionate and somehow even intimate at times, when it feels like a cosy conversation with a friend.' EVA-CHRISTIE BESSALA, DIRECTOR, GLOBAL CLIENTS PRICING AND PROCUREMENT, PWC

'A highly practical handbook that covers a range of important topics and explores them thoughtfully, intelligently and with emotion. *Begin With You* appreciates that mental health is a sensitive, sometimes challenging and very personal topic, and I would recommend this book to the novice, practitioner and expert alike.' SHAUN DAVIS, GROUP DIRECTOR, HEALTH, SAFETY AND WELL-BEING, BELRON INTERNATIONAL

'To be invited into the world and shoes that Petra Velzeboer has walked in is such a privilege, as it allows the reader to pause and be amazed at the courage it has taken for this brave woman to come out the other end with such beauty, compassion and a zest for life to be the best version of herself. The tips and wise words are like "pick-me-up pills" that will help all those that read her journey. Thank you for sharing your incredible story with us.' KAMEL HOTHI OBE, NON-EXECUTIVE DIRECTOR, TLC LIONS

Begin With You

Invest in your mental well-being and satisfaction at work

Petra Velzeboer

KoganPage

Publisher's note
Every possible effort has been made to ensure that the information contained in this book is accurate at the time of going to press, and the publisher and author cannot accept responsibility for any errors or omissions, however caused. No responsibility for loss or damage occasioned to any person acting, or refraining from action, as a result of the material in this publication can be accepted by the editor, the publisher or the author.

First published in Great Britain and the United States in 2023 by Kogan Page Limited

2nd Floor, 45 Gee Street	8 W 38th Street, Suite 902	4737/23 Ansari Road
London	New York, NY 10018	Daryaganj
EC1V 3RS	USA	New Delhi 110002
United Kingdom		India

www.koganpage.com

Kogan Page books are printed on paper from sustainable forests.

© Petra Velzeboer, 2023

The right of Petra Velzeboer to be identified as the author of this work has been asserted by her in accordance with the Copyright, Designs and Patents Act 1988.

ISBNs
Hardback   978 1 3986 1033 0
Paperback   978 1 3986 1031 6
Ebook   978 1 3986 1032 3

British Library Cataloguing-in-Publication Data
A CIP record for this book is available from the British Library.

Library of Congress Control Number
2023001132

Typeset by Integra Software Services, Pondicherry
Print production managed by Jellyfish
Printed and bound by CPI Group (UK) Ltd, Croydon, CR0 4YY

To my younger self
and all those who thought they couldn't stand...
We're still standing!

You've got this!

Contents

Foreword

During the safety briefing on an aircraft the air steward will ask you to put your own oxygen mask on before helping others. In the frenetic and fast moving VUCA world that we all live in today – where is your oxygen mask? Have you put it on yourself first? I suspect not!

My own crucible moment came in 2008, when I was diagnosed with anxiety-fuelled depression and my subsequent purpose-filled journey over the last 10 years has taught me that health and well-being must be the most important priority in my life. What is more important than your physical, emotional, mental and spiritual health? Nothing is more important than protecting this valuable asset.

Having said that, we all too often fail to prioritise our health. We will often find a reason not to go for that walk, or not to connect with a loved one or nature. It's not easy to be constantly mindful of what we eat and drink, or to ensure that we get enough sleep each night. Why? Maybe we just don't know what to do. It all seems too difficult and time consuming.

This quote from Joyce Sunada has really stuck with me:

> If you don't make time for your wellness, you will be forced to make time for your illness.

Making a habit of protecting your health and embarking upon activities that will enhance your health can be daunting and stressful in itself. Finding the motivation and discipline to go for a run on a cold, grey wintry evening can be very difficult.

However, we can only care for the well-being and mental health of others if we care for our own, and so it all begins with you!

This book will provide some very valuable insights on how to protect your mental health and well-being, and in so doing become a champion for mental health.

Petra's very honest account of her own struggles and how her breakdown has led to a breakthrough in her life will be an inspiration to many. This book is not only an inspiration, it also offers some real practical strategies to employ as individuals as we all look for ways to enhance and protect our mental health. In addition, it is a book of hope for those who may be struggling and need to know that recovery is possible and living a fulfilling life is possible.

It's an honour to have the opportunity to contribute to this book, and I trust it will touch the lives of many individuals: those that are well and looking to maintain their health as well as those who struggle on a daily basis, and who will find hope and inspiration in Petra's story and wisdom.

Geoff McDonald
Co-Founder, Minds@Work and Board Adviser, Supernova
Former Global VP Human Resources, Unilever

Introduction

What's all the fuss about mental health – and what in the world does it have to do with your career? Well, if you've picked up this book you're likely to have faced a crash point at some time in your life. From sheer exhaustion to a feeling of emptiness in your personal rat race, to burnout, anxiety, depression and a whole host of other challenges.

You might be an entrepreneur like me, addicted to the hustle, to your legacy and have bought into the Silicon Valley dream that if you just work hard enough maybe you'll become a unicorn and be able to put your feet up on top of your mountains of wealth.

You might be climbing up the career ladder, pushing for status or you might be representing a cause, which on top of your daily workload has left you feeling overwhelmed and questioning what it's really all about.

We live in a society that is all about the next thing, celebrates striving and tells you that everyone else is just doing things a little better than you. We are trapped in a cult of busy and only take drastic measures to change things when our body or mind has reached a limit that is affecting our health. We wait until crisis to change and we wonder why it takes us so long to recover from the build-up that's been going on in our body for years.

While the world of work is changing, there will still be countless numbers of you hiding your mental health diagnosis in shame, mentally masked-up at work acting as if everything is OK, secretly struggling to not show up in any way other than you always have. Our society perpetuates the notion that toughness wins while investing in your well-being means slowing down, losing your edge or being weak.

Now, I'd like to tell you that I'm always the picture of good health. That I've hacked the balance needed in a noisy distraction-filled world and have built my career with myself at the core always and that my wisdom is the perfect formula for success. The reality is that my life has gone back-to-front and the challenges I've faced have forced me to consider this topic in a serious way in order to sustain success long term and not crash in trauma-induced burnout, addiction and workaholism.

I have dedicated the last 15 years of my life to understanding myself and training as a psychotherapist, gaining an MSc in psychodynamics of human development, studying coaching, organizational change and working with countless organizations on their strategy for well-being at work.

While it's great that there's more awareness, so many people are still getting this wrong!

Much of the health industry is stuck in the dark ages and simply isn't adapting as fast as the world is around us. We divide our physical health from our mental health, treating symptoms separately rather than connecting the dots of everything that's going on together. The mental health space labels people readily, gives out antidepressants like they're candy but doesn't look at the impact of our environment, isolation in cities, fear in the media, technology addictions and our nutritional decline and sedentary lifestyles, which are playing a part in how we feel.

Even talking therapies can keep us in a fixed state, telling our story over and over without acknowledging developments in neuroscience that suggest that time spent imagining a different future can actually help us get there better than circling our past for endless clues.

Gone is the idea that our brain is fixed by the time we're 25 and instead, when we think new thoughts and do new things that can feel effortful or make us uncomfortable, we can learn, grow and heal our brain – making anything possible.

Wouldn't this mean that your diagnosis of depression or anxiety isn't a fixed state, but instead is your body giving you information that something needs to change? More than any of these things, many of us give away our agency to anyone we perceive as an authority. This might mean if a doctor tells us to take an antidepressant we go ahead and do it, numbing further any agency we have in changing our environment, thoughts or reality. A therapist keeps us in a loop telling our story for years and we go along with it even though we leave every session feeling triggered and terrible.

Please don't get me wrong. I am all for medical intervention, mental health support and talking therapies – I am a therapist myself and have experienced therapy as a client, as well as taken antidepressants at times in my life. We need to know our story in order to understand ourselves, learn about our minds and create space away from being flooded by emotion and feeling, to be able to do the things we need to do to improve and manage our mental health.

However, what I'm seeing around me is a mental health crisis that has reached epic proportions: one where even the well-being narrative has become saturated with influencers, overwhelmed with gurus and confusing in its solutions and narratives. From coaches who all have the three-step solution to changing your life, to therapies that are confusing and will all tell you something different, to lifestyles that are claustrophobic, with pressure and advice that will make your well-being to-do list longer than your work to-do list – and creating a feeling of failure if you haven't done all the things you *should* do in order to recover from the life you find yourself in.

This book shows you a different way. That mental health doesn't mean taking a slower path, being unable to build a legacy or needing to take a back seat in the world. In fact, understanding your mental health and taking radical responsibility for it can be your superpower and allow you to create a legacy on top of your legacy – one that is meaningful, powerful and allows us to build a better work world.

I, like you, want to achieve greatness. I want to build a legacy that lasts, I want to create impact and I'd like to think I have a phenomenal work ethic. AND, I know if I don't prioritize my well-being and mental health – over time my path will be skewed, I'll numb out my feelings, hurt my body and crash out – leaving a ripple effect of pain in the people around me!

I want to help you redefine what success looks like for you and give you insights and tools to invest in your mental health in order to build workplace cultures of the future, enable you to enjoy the journey and create the legacy that matters.

I want to show you that no matter what situation you're in you can assess where you're at, learn about your brain, decide where you want to go and take the action necessary to get there. There are some key reasons why I know the things I know – my own story of challenge and learning to manage my own brain, my vast experience as a mental health professional listening to hundreds of clients, as well as working as a thought leader in this wonderful new world of work. All of these have given me information that can help you not only manage your experience of life, but also maybe have a little fun with it!

With all that said, sometimes I feel like I still give my thoughts away to the highest bidder.

My nervous system dictates the decisions I make, the choices on offer and my entire world view is just set up to keep me safe.

But safe from what – truly living? What does that even look like in this bubble-wrapped world, dripping fear into my nervous system so I think the life I'm in is fully mine when it was never mine to begin with.

I've thought long and hard about what I want to say versus what I should say on these pages. It's kept me up at night! I've weighed up all the advice – just get published (it almost doesn't matter what you say), write to get on bigger stages (also doesn't really matter what you say), sensation-alize your story (someone will want to be voyeuristic) – and I'm left with a few thoughts.

It kind of doesn't matter what these words say because they are just a small piece in the giant puzzle that is your life.

And…

For me, it matters that I say something!

To seep through the world of noise and that helpless feeling I'm seeing everywhere.

Where mental health is a buzzword, but we've lost the ability to just be real.

Where our apps and technology give us access to profes-sionals wherever we are and yet we're living more depressed and anxious lives.

Where the workplace of the future is meant to be a haven of trust and well-being and yet we still outsource mental health to benefits and helplines, uncomfortable with having real and honest conversations ourselves.

A world where we focus on time and productivity in a hybrid world but have lost our grip on connection and a feeling of belonging.

Where the mental health narrative, in my opinion, is steeped in negativity and we focus on talking about not being OK without truly understanding what could make us thrive – yes, even in this changing world where most media is telling us what an awful world we're living in!

The thing I want to say…

The thing that is screaming through my body is that we're getting this mental health and well-being business all wrong. We're focused on the wrong places, getting more and more lost and stuck, living out our trauma identities in a system that perpetuates our trauma identities. We're looking for hacks, tactics and tips – reducing the complexity of our brain to 30-second hits of greatness, hoping that by stringing the shorts together we'll have a life well lived, free from anxiety, melancholy and paradox.

In theory we have more freedom than we've ever had, however we still seem to be living out society's version of who we should be and I wonder, I just wonder, if anyone's life is truly theirs? I wonder if the surge in anxiety, depression and a host of other challenges is each of us questioning who we are, truly recognizing the shortness of life and asking ourselves – sometimes unconsciously through physical and mental health symptoms – is this the life we really want?

My own questions are connected to my upbringing of course – how, even with the knowledge I have, I can give away my thoughts to the highest bidder and be influenced by others' views of how I should live my life.

Due to my extreme story, which you'll read about in the next chapter; I see the world through a lens that perhaps not everyone sees – I see how media influence and group-think are affecting our mental health more than we realize. I see people giving away their decision-making power all the time and then wondering why their body is reacting with signs and symptoms of poor physical or mental health and I have a theory, which I will outline in this book. I believe the amount we give away our agency – even to therapists, coaches, bosses or well-meaning family – has a direct correlation to some of the mental health issues I see rampant in individuals and workplaces.

I will highlight how we are just scratching the surface of understanding the beautiful information mechanism that is your body and mind. That deep down in the recesses of your mind you know what you need and that sometimes that knowledge is scary – because it means you must take radical responsibility for your life, your influences, friendships and yes, even your job.

When this knowledge scares us (even unconsciously) we tend to do anything in our power to distract ourselves from this truth – after all, change is scary, especially if we are totally responsible for how things go and can't blame why things didn't work on a coach, adviser or well-being professional.

And so, we medicate, complain and zone out from the big questions in favour of energy spent consumed by the woes of the world, we take sides politically or have bold opinions about everyone else's life without doing the work that would improve ours!

We try to imitate what we perceive to be others' fast-paced route to success without realizing that this pursuit is stifling our breath and could even be slowly killing us.

And so we paint a picture of a good life on Instagram and struggle for the success that is financial or in other ways acceptable to society. So as the world accelerates around us we struggle to adapt to this increasing pace, giving away our thoughts to the highest bidder as we become more frantic in our daily business and desperately just want to feel like we belong. So our influences become society, family, religion, bosses, influencers and algorithms, and all the while our body is telling us something different – that there's something gravely wrong and if we don't listen it will tell us in bigger and bigger ways – and yet, we trundle along in our little lives following what everyone else sees as best for us.

I will explore this topic in this book and hopefully give you a measure of yourself and a new way to contemplate success and the tools you'll need to make sure your body and mind are intact when you get there. Not to give you Instagrammable hacks to make you feel better about yourself but to help you simply think for yourself and decide for yourself what it is you need!

As the apocryphal quote attributed to Albert Einstein says, 'Education is not the learning of facts, but the training of the mind to think', and I realize now that this is the thought that I want to echo, this is the thing I want to say – I want to remind you to think for yourself.

In a world of self-help, information overload, hacks, technology and advice, I wonder if the biggest problem is that we've been collectively giving our power away and forgetting how to think for ourselves. Maybe a new world of work and a view on mental health is much simpler than we think. Maybe learning to think for ourselves is the most profound approach to well-being – not thought that is overrun with other people's ideas but thought that is ours – separate from the noise and simply true for us.

I realize this is actually a tall order. How do we even think for ourselves? How do we know what is a true, original thought and what is just influenced by our past, our nervous system, our friends and the world around us?

What we want more than anything is to belong.

From the beginning of time, belonging signalled our chance of survival. If you think of historic tribes, to be cast out or alone often meant dying of starvation or being more at risk from predators. It did us well to play by the rules and stick with groupthink.

These days, we have more means of survival on our own than ever before, evidenced by 8.3 million people living alone in the UK (Clark, 2022) and approximately 37 million in the US (United States Census Bureau, 2021); we no longer need the tribe to meet our basic needs of food, safety and shelter.

And yet, there's a hangover from our past.

Humans have been known to change their values and behaviours just to fit in and feel like they belong. Think of your time at school when you joined in with the bullies or did something you now view as shameful just to fit in with the popular kids – the world of work is often an echo of these experiences.

In order to get promoted, keep my salary intact and avoid embarrassment or shame, I may adapt my values and behaviours to belong.

In a world of mental health crisis, Johann Hari (2019) gives us a new lens on our survival needs when he states that 'every one of the social and psychological causes of depression and anxiety they have discovered has something in common. They are all forms of disconnection.'

So, what is the line between the healthy connection that we need to improve our mental health and giving our power away in order to fit in and survive? How can we separate our survival instincts, which can make us adapt who we are so fundamentally in order to fit in, from our ability to stand alone in our truth?

What is true belonging – the kind that will improve our mental health? As Dr Brené Brown so beautifully puts it in her book *Braving the Wilderness* (2019), true belonging doesn't require that we change who we are, it requires that we be who we are!

What does this have to do with our mental health and the skyrocketing challenge that is society? I believe that it is the very act of giving our agency away that is crashing our mental health statistics. Fitting in, conforming, adhering, labelling, fixing is all part of the problem masquerading as part of the solution. While there may be a place for all of these things if you (being the only expert on your experience) feel like it makes sense, the overarching plastering of solutions and shaming if it doesn't work for you is driving us to become sheep, focusing on signs and symptoms rather than systemic avoidance of the actual issues.

Have I got you on side yet? Probably not. You may be reading these marginally interesting words, telling yourself that you definitely think for yourself, have created the life you want and are just trying to take care of this tiny problem that is a thorn in the side of your perfect life – from anxious thinking, physical pain and melancholy to depression or even a range of symptoms linked to a mental health diagnosis. If you could just hack those you'd be good and just one more book, course, meditation, trauma bond insight or therapy session will give you what you need. But what if it doesn't, when does it end? What does good look like? What is the end result you're looking for and what if there were no end result – is this how you would live your life? Is this how you would approach work?

> Thinking for yourself is the thing on which everything else depends. (Nancy Kline, *Time to Think*, 2002)

This book is for anyone who wants a new lens on the mental health narrative.

It's for anyone who has tried so many things and yet still finds themselves struggling. It's for you if you're sick of self-help books and hacks and want instead a true and lasting lens through which to live your life. It's for you if you're sick and tired of being sick and tired and want instead a lesson on bravery so that you can do the things that only you know you can do – things that may just radically change the trajectory and experience of your life.

In this book I'll tell you a bit about my story of growing up in a cult steeped in groupthink, what I did to get out of it and how I changed my own life from alcohol-addicted depressive into one that is successful to me.

I'll help you think about success through a new lens and highlight why I believe our current approach to mental health is wrong. I'll touch on some key principles when it comes to groupthink and the influences around us that are impacting our well-being negatively, and crucially, I'll give you some tools to help you think for yourself.

I'll outline some of the key challenges facing many of us today including stress and overwork, anxiety, depression and burnout, offering you resources and tools to learn about what's going on for you, thereby giving you the tools to think for yourself and set you on a path to reducing your symptoms and improving your life.

Of course it's one thing to learn about a concept and quite another to maintain a good life long term. Just like walking requires one foot in front of the other and a constant balancing act, I'll show you how taking responsibility for your thinking and overall well-being takes maintenance and balance – something that can be so intrinsic to our lifestyle so we don't even need to think about it – and yet, like a toddler just pulling themselves up onto their feet, it takes a little bit of practice to get there.

I also want to highlight the key skills necessary to supporting others. The question I am asked the most is 'How can I best help my colleague/friend/partner/child, who I can see is struggling?' More of you want to know how you can help others in a useful way and there are some key principles that can help you provide others with space to think and act for themselves.

In Chapter 7 I'll outline the new world of work and what it takes to create change. Internal activism and channelling your passion and frustration into useful action rather than becoming overwhelmed, burnt out and leaving your job. Of course understanding what is toxic and unchangeable is also a key insight into improving your mental health and I'll show you how to assess where you are to help you know what's right for you.

I'll leave you with key principles to help you think for yourself, which can influence every aspect of your life for good if you just cultivate the bravery necessary to live your life – not anyone else's! That, my friends, in my opinion, is the key to living a mentally healthy life.

This is a book about learning to be brave.

And if my story is anything to go by, bravery doesn't usually feel brave. It feels like desperation, necessity and a drive for hope.

Bravery, however, isn't just something a few people are born with. I'm pleased to note that bravery is a skill that can be developed over time, through practice and neuro-plasticity – our brain's ability to reorganize connections in response to learning or experience.

Let's figure out together how to make that happen so you, like me, can learn to live a great life no matter what is in your past.

CHAPTER ONE

Why me?

I've done a few things in my time. I've been involved in youth mental health, I'm a psychotherapist, I have a Master's degree and I'm CEO of PVL, a company focused on workplace mental health. I've also had the privilege of telling my story and sharing my thoughts as a global keynote and TEDx speaker, I have two beautiful teenagers, a beautiful partner and home, and I love my job and my life!

I was also born into a notorious religious cult where I grew up thinking the world was going to end, didn't go to school and I have experienced trauma that has left me living with PTSD. It took 22 years for me to be free physically and it's a lifelong journey to be free mentally – to learn to think for myself.

I've been asked many times to write a memoir because my life was just that weird that it might be interesting – but the truth is, I don't trust my memory to accurately chronologize the whole series of events. I've probably blocked some of it out but also there was so much change so frequently that I'm bound to tell the story wrong, to mash it into a collective experience of emotional turmoil and questions so as to make a great story but probably confuse the reader in its twists and turns.

To be honest, I'm probably scared of re-traumatizing myself. Blowing up my current life as I drag up the memory of my former one and judging myself for being self-indulgent in the telling. The truth of the matter is that once I started telling my story to others (or at least bits of it) I realized that I wasn't that special anyway – everyone has a story. Everyone has conditioning, expectations, neurosis, hurt, drama, pain and self-doubt and I'm just a human with a cocktail of all of those things – trying to find my way in a complex world. Trying to find purpose and meaning amidst pressure and senselessness. We are all the same at the heart of it, managing our mental health amidst pressures to survive in a society that wants to tell us how to live.

There are, however, bits of my story that are important to tell so you can understand how I've come to my thoughts and what I want this book to say. I haven't just plucked this thinking out of thin air but have had half a life experiencing the opposite of free thinking, on the extreme end of conformity and groupthink, fighting to be free.

Only to find that freedom can be masked as being absorbed into other ways of conformity, it's subtle and sneaky and is a thread through all of life and society – fuelling the mental health crisis we see today.

So where did it all start?

The cult (if you must know) was known originally as The Children of God and has gone through a multitude of rebrands, known more recently as The Family International. Google will show you the dark side of free love, child abuse, oppressive propaganda and a tribe of people prepared for the world to end – morphing into my generation impacted by trauma, trying to survive in a world we weren't given the tools for, often struggling in addiction, developing chronic mental health issues and a multitude of preventable suicides.

That's not the lens through which I see my childhood though, even if it informs my hindsight view of the experience.

I remember lots of joy. I remember music, collective purpose, excitement and knowing that I was born to be part of something. That I was born special.

The Children of God was formed in the 1970s when a multitude of movements sprung up off the back of hippy searching, LSD-informed questioning and a generation of people reacting to the Vietnam war and wondering if they could think for themselves and decide on a different way to live. One such movement started with a charismatic preacher named David Berg who had tried to fit into his mother's evangelistic view of Christianity – he was probably always in her shadow and was always trying to make a name for himself. The narrative I was raised on detailed a lost teacher stuck in the boundaries of religion, desperately trying to find a purer more truthful way to live, which then informed a movement. But history now tells us he was kicked out of the church for sexual deviance, used his teenage kids to build a dream and subsequently built a whole belief system as a way to validate his sexual deviances, thereby traumatizing an entire generation of children.

I never met David Berg but he was brought to life daily through comic books, was affectionately known as 'Grandpa' and celebrated as the holder of all wisdom through his teachings that spanned the nuance of when to take a shit, how to be free sexually, what the afterlife would be like and the daily practices of living a purposeful life.

Long before I knew what the word *elite* meant, I was born into an *elite generation* that was special – that was meant to save the world. I say this because happiness, as told in Mo Gawdat's book *Solve for Happy* (2017) describes evidence of happiness as expectations needing to match experience – when you're born knowing you are just that unique and special, to find out you're just a regular plain-Jane human being in later life is such a perceived fall from grace as to plummet one's mental health into depression and senselessness. A fate many of my generation experienced – but more on the aftermath later.

This is the bit I always get stuck on because I don't want to give this man any more airtime. I don't want *my* words used to describe *him* (the founder, Berg) or his belief system – instead I want to focus on what it took to keep my generation alive, and crucially, I want words to translate what I experienced into our world of groupthink and the mental health agenda I see today. I want to say something that will matter to you, that will help you think for yourself and decide how to live a good, successful and mentally healthy life – even if you have a diagnosis, skewed expectations of who you are in the world or a story that you never want to put down in words.

Having said that, my publishers say I cannot just start in the middle of the story, I have to give you a little bit of context so that it makes sense in your head and not just mine – so here goes.

David Berg theorized that a generation protected from the influences of groupthink (which he claimed started in the education system) would be protected from being moulded into society's view of what life should be and would be able to think for themselves, being unique in their ability to observe the system for what it was and thereby bring conviction into a new way of life.

My generation was a lab experiment.

We were supposed to prove his theory that to be sheltered from *the system* would bring enlightenment not only to our own pure generation but also to a troubled world. Of course, what ended up happening is that we traded in one kind of groupthink for another. We couldn't just be sheltered from one thing and left open to our own thoughts, instead we had to be indoctrinated with his thoughts, with a new view on what our purpose, thoughts and actions should be.

In order to protect us from thinking for ourselves, the structures and belief systems became more and more complex, always with the notion that our thoughts could not be trusted. While we were protected from evil thoughts of the 'other', we couldn't just be an 'empty vessel' – which essentially meant we weren't guarding our thoughts astutely enough – we had to be brave enough to indoctrinate ourselves with his radical and prophetic world view: spirituality translated by a man building himself up to be a guru, the one true prophet, with a whole philosophy of identity, practice and purpose.

We were raised to be willing to die for our faith.

To hold true no matter what.

There are recordings out there of children from the cult who'd been taken away from their parents and interviewed by social services. Pre-dawn raids where police took children away, hoping to find hard evidence of abuse, to interview us to find our parents unfit to look after us, to rescue us from our toxic environments, and it's interesting to see our training come into play. What the police and social services hadn't factored in was how well we would have rehearsed this very thing. This test of our faith that we could pass or fail. To fail was to be seen as weak, to let our entire community down and, worse than that, to be seen as the weak link, the crack in the armour of an army.

When we were as young as six, we were saying that we were making the world a better place, that there was no abuse in our communities, and we were home-schooled to such a high standard that to take us away from our families would be the real abuse.

We were speaking our truth because to be raised in our version of normal was to say we wouldn't have identified with abuse as a phrase – it was just our normal. Not going to school, living in a sexualized environment, believing the world would end, doing army drills, reading Berg's propaganda first thing every morning, seeing our peers punished or made an example of, moving country in the dead of night, all of this was pitched as part of the excitement of being *this* special and unique.

We were privileged to experience a different life and it was *them* on the other side, in the system that had gotten it all wrong. Cartoons of zombie-like children tapped into the worldly education system being fed lies was a common thread of our messaging. Isn't it interesting that in order to take the light of blame off one's own situation, it makes more sense to shine that same light onto someone else – we see it in politics, media and business every day.

In some ways, cults are like corporates. They often start with a charismatic founder, inspiring people to join them on limited pay on the promise of later reward (e.g. equity in the biz), the promise of community and building something special. People love being part of a purposeful dream where they may just rise to the top, but it's later, once the seed of something special grows roots and there are more people involved, that we realize we can no longer be a hapless movement for change – we now need to organize.

We need structure, policies, rules, hiring and firing practices, and that dreaded level – middle management.

This is the layer that now holds the power for delivering the message from the founder, for putting into practice those rules and structures, for spending time with the people who believe in the dream. This is also where ego, power, control and all manner of human flaws can ascend to the surface and influence the overall culture and the human experience on the ground.

This is how a variety of experiences across the globe developed within the cult. Some of my generation's memories are broadly good, filled with purpose, daily community practices that gave off a feeling of stability and contentment – everyone had a role, everyone knew their place, which made the cogs turn in the wider machine that was still *special* and there to save the world. Even sweeping a floor had the gravitas of something that was meaningful to the wider purpose – just like I imagine writing a line of code at Apple probably has the feeling of playing a part in the dream (or at least it used to).

So, what was my experience within all of this? A mixed bag really.

I grew up in a blended family – my mother has three daughters from three different men and while pregnant with her third child she met my stepfather (who would be the greatest father figure I could have). Seemingly overnight we became a family of seven living in a commune out in Brazil, and the more time passes, the more I realize I don't know enough about my parents' experience or their reasoning for the choices they made. The older I get, the more mysteries emerge, so to stay on track and away from the rabbit hole of psychoanalysing my parents, I should say that I loved having siblings and felt a protective presence in my father, which in a world of free love was a privilege I can only now truly recognize.

Over time my parents became leaders within the community and travelled extensively between *homes* (aka communes of varying sizes) leaving us within the organized structures of the commune – run somewhat like a school, children and young people were put together in groups by age, often sleeping in dorms together and going through the day with every minute scheduled so you always knew what was expected of you.

I guess because my parents would sometimes sneak time between travels to just be alone with us kids, the story I tell myself is that we were always a strong family unit within the wider landscape of single mothers, kids who didn't know their fathers and families separated across continents. As more time passes, I doubt how much of that is true and whether it's just a narrative I've become comfortable with to make me OK with things that weren't OK.

As my parents were away a lot, I remember not having someone to go to if something felt difficult. Emotions were not encouraged if they didn't fit into how we *should* feel based on what was good for the group. There was no space to cry (unless you were so moved by the Lord), no room to be angry (unless you wanted justice against the system) and definitely no room to think for yourself (question anything that was going on and you would be punished) – these were the implicit rules and I survived this environment by being as invisible as possible. I know now that suppressing our emotions and not having an outlet is one of the key factors to blame for skyrocketing rates of mental health issues globally. When we have traumatic experiences (including bullying, financial troubles, racism, loss, loneliness or mental health issues) and keep our feelings inside, we tell ourselves we are the only ones in the world who feel that way and this hopeless isolation can drive people to do the unthinkable. To feel and to be open about our stories in environments that are safe and without judgement is key to leading mentally healthy lives and any organization that prioritizes collective and individual well-being needs to allow its members to be visible, to have a voice and to feel safe to show emotion without judgement.

When I was 13 the founder, David Berg, died (finally, I can stop giving him a direct voice on these pages!) and a new era would arise. I remember 80 of us cramming into a double living room to listen to the big news – he was dead! He got old, heaven took him, whatever. I remember my nervous energy as I wondered what would be next and the *letters* were read aloud with a carefully curated message to keep the masses from riot. Berg's wife Maria and her lover Peter were now *crowned* King and Queen of the cult. We no longer had to live in giant homes that took a ridiculous amount of organization to run, but for all intents and purposes were trusted with more freedom (aka God had now decided it was OK), could decide for ourselves how to live while still reading their propaganda (or 'God's word' as they would refer to it) and staying focused on our mission through their anointed guidance.

Prophecy was now a major force and David Berg would be leading us from the *other* side (so much for being done giving him a voice!). I just remember quite quickly moving into a small three-bedroom flat with my parents and four siblings in Belgium. This was the first time we'd lived alone as a family, no other people besides us, and none of us really knew the rules of engagement – including my parents. My parents put on a strong front but I'm pretty sure they were just making it up as they went along. I think they had a mixture of benefits and some money given to them as leaders to continue visiting the smaller homes to assess how they were doing and give them guidance on how to adjust to this new way... I realize now it was the blind leading the blind. How could they help with anything that they were making up themselves?

Over the next few years I would realize just how weird I was.

My mother wanted us to stay busy and nurture some interests, so I remember taking a dance class and my siblings trying out other things. I was awkward and unhappy and didn't know how to engage in this world – the world we were taught was our enemy, trying at every turn to trap us in its oppressive thinking, we were now meant to engage with as friends and I know I hated myself but wasn't sure what was normal teenage angst and what was God's punishment. This was when I got my first library card – a gateway into the experience of humanity!

Having a library card was exciting and somewhat illicit. Go into a building and get free books – this was like heaven come to earth as it opened an entire world of experience to me! We were raised on biblical stories, heroic fighters, Christians being eaten by lions for their faith (we would be asked 'would you be willing to do this too?' and we could only say yes!) and now I had an unsupervised gateway into learning and the wider human experience.

I was interested in angsty poetry steeped in human emotion, in coming-of-age stories infused with trauma, exploring alternative sexualities, drugs and consciousness-expanding experiences, dynamic questions about life and global experience.

I can't describe what independent reading did for me. I would take out the maximum amount of books allowed and hide the more risqué ones. If discovered, I would tell people that God told me to understand people more deeply so I could save them. I was fascinated by emotive language as it gave me words for otherwise confused feelings and it simultaneously made me wonder at everything I'd ever been told.

I couldn't have formed this full thought then, but the seeds to these questions were planted – was it possible for people to truly think for themselves and what was truth – could there be another way to live?

Without this book becoming fully autobiographical, let me bring this full circle. My own mental health crisis and what I learnt along the way, coupled with my studies and experience as a mental health professional, has given me a lens with which I can hopefully provide support and guidance for the challenges you face in your life. As this is only my lens, it's crucial that you try my ideas on for size, see how they fit, and then decide, through your own lens of experience, what is true for you and which bits to discard!

If you take nothing else away from this book then take this – in an age of information overload, even within the well-being and mental health space – it is more crucial than ever to learn to think for yourself!

We all are conditioned to think through the lens of our own upbringing, religion, culture, media and family dynamics, and the real coming of age (no matter what age you are) is to figure out how to understand those roots and then intentionally nurture who you want to become – my aim is to give you a few ways to try to do that, like a parent pushing you along with training wheels in order for you to then tread your own path.

We often don't understand the impact of our conditioned upbringing until we're in a physical or mental health crisis. We may see ourselves as tough, resilient survivors who experienced difficulties but nothing that bad and look, we studied, worked, made money – whatever it is. That's our evidence that we're OK.

Until we're not OK.

No matter how resilient you are, you too can experience the long-term impacts of trauma, the stacking of stress in your body, burnout, poor mental health, overwork or overwhelm triggered seemingly by one thing – a life event such as the end of a relationship or a job breakdown, financial difficulties, bereavement, a child with challenges, etc.

It's never just that one thing though. It's a lifetime of challenges stacked on top of each other with that one thing being the straw that breaks the proverbial camel's back.

And so for me, it stacked and it stacked until I tumbled.

At 16 I left my parents in Belgium and went to a big commune in Switzerland. I went to be a glamorous secretary to a leader (my one skill was typing 120 words a minute) and when I arrived in a home filled with other teenagers, excited that finally my life would begin, I was told that my glamorous role was no longer viable – however, they needed someone to run the kitchen for 100 people.

I'd never done more than cook an egg for breakfast. They said not to worry, that I would have help – of course I wouldn't do it alone and it would be a great blessing to the Lord if I would sacrifice for the cause. It wouldn't be for long, maybe a month or two and then the secretary job would open up again and I could continue my glamorous trajectory (this was how I heard it in my head anyway).

The reality was that I'd arrived, they'd used God as part of their persuasion technique and now I was doing the *right* thing and running a kitchen at 16 years old.

This building was originally set up as a school and had a large industrial kitchen – the biggest appliances I'd ever seen in my life. I had no idea what I was doing and have blanked out my original feeling of overwhelm as I stared at the confused pantry filled with donated goods and the schedule that meant three meals a day must be served for 100 people. I was 16. I remember organizing people to chop, prepare and cook. There wasn't any Google to find recipes and so I made things up – I was to blame for some of the awful meals that would be put out to my peers. Once everything was served, I would often hide, in the pantry, or stay outside; I would overeat to find comfort, I would pray that I would pass this test.

I did this for a year and this experience acted as an exit strategy for further excitement. Given how much *freedom* people apparently had, there were more and more *bad apples* and so they created youth camps. The parable told by Berg was that one bad apple could rot the barrel, so any dissent from groupthink was seen as a serious threat to our way of life and had to urgently be nipped in the bud (excuse the mixed metaphor). The aim was to get teenagers together to inspire them to continue the fight our parents started, to make examples of dissenters and to indoctrinate us with the new radicalized message.

The legend of our parents' generation was thrilling to me. Steeped in possibility, mission and shared purpose – I thought being in the kitchen might be a test. If I didn't complain (have a voice) and got on with what was required of me, I might just be rewarded in being part of the chosen few who would bring that legend back into our lifetime. Our belief system was steeped in words like sacrifice and reward, so whenever something wasn't to our liking it wasn't an opportunity for change or for making new choices, it was our time to sacrifice our own desires and thoughts to the wiser good. The environment was rife for power imbalance and abuse even though there were good people who had good intentions throughout.

Just like cults can be like corporates – I see a similar belief system impacting people's well-being on a daily basis. If you just sacrifice yourself now, turn a blind eye to the toxicity, question nothing, show up, head down, get the work done and pretend you have agency by picking a political side or having a dinner-party opinion – you will be rewarded with a bigger salary, a mortgage and a promise of a better life.

Just hold on.

One day soon.

One day soon was my life path. So, from the kitchens in one commune, I got to do the kitchens at the youth camps across Europe. This was a step up. I would be on the periphery of greatness observing the celebrities playing music on stage, telling stories, prophesying and getting our generation back on track.

I was only a teenager myself but this is when the seed of youth work was planted. The troublemakers were sent to the kitchen (I lived the punishment every day, yet they visited to peel piles of potatoes for not 80 people but hundreds in order to get back on track to deserving the Lord's blessing in the form of socializing, dances and truth) and I listened and talked.

You'll be OK.
It's only a season in your life.
Thank you for helping – you are amazing.
Et cetera. Et cetera.

I travelled across Europe, one camp after another, feeling like I was one step closer to the mission I was born to create. With this first year of fully being away from my siblings, there were plenty of coming-of-age memories, friends were made, some sense of self was discovered but mostly I was angsty, shy and feeling very much like an outsider of the clique of cool kids that seemed to be running the show.

While I'm trying to translate my experience into normal words that you will all understand there were plenty of things that you may find bizarre as well. I remember one particular day after a youth camp, I was sleeping in the dorm with maybe 10 other teenagers and we could hear an amateur exorcism going on downstairs. We must all have been pretending to be asleep while they were shouting and praying in tongues in the effort to fight off a demon. I remember piercing the silence to ask if people were awake and a murmur of yesses came from all corners of the dark room.

I remember feeling distinctly that something wasn't quite right and that the room needed comforting – within my shy self my rescuing behaviours and early leadership skills were somehow surfacing. I said something comforting and somehow reassuring – I echoed all I knew and said that we didn't understand everything and that sometimes God's plan felt confusing so, if we felt confused, then that was a sign that things were probably right (groupthink had twisted my confusion and my discomfort into a belief that there was something wrong with *me*. That I should shut up and play my part). There would be so many things I echoed that were a product of groupthink but which I rationalized would help people feel better and so I was a minion of Berg's ghostly voice.

There was one New Year's Eve when the matron insisted that we take part in a 'candlelight service' where we would take turns to confess our shortcomings and itemize some goals for the new year. It would take hours for all 80 of us to take turns, so I bravely spoke up to suggest that we should instead confess our sins simultaneously (surely Jesus could hear us all at once). My heart pounded in my throat and my suggestion was quickly shot down.

I was reminded of my place.

But there were moments like these that are dotted throughout my teenage years. Something in my body forcing me to have a voice, say something, stand up to groupthink and then feel shame or repress why I did it, storing it away until it would all stack together to make a bigger statement. That statement would build into resentment, anger and depression covered over by alcohol addiction and excuses – trying to numb the rage I had at not having a voice, but also not knowing how to use the voice I would later have.

I see so many people now in a world that makes it so easy to distract and numb, avoiding how they truly feel for years and years only to have this suppression seep out into physical and mental health issues, unable to be kept wrapped beneath the surface any longer. They go to doctors to be told they have a chemical imbalance, are depressed or anxious when really their body is just shouting out to them to live a different life, to truly say what is inside of them!

Another key feature that shaped me was the amount of cruel and unusual punishment that went on throughout my childhood and in this place I called home. In the 1980s and 90s corporal punishment wasn't that surprising no matter where you were but what was unique was the cult's ability to make examples of people. Public spanks with paddles or belts in front of your peers ensured everyone benefited from God's lessons and everyone played a part in bringing this person onto the 'right path'. If you were considered out of line or said something humorous, you would have to wear a large sign hung around your neck saying 'I am on silence restriction', which could last for weeks and meant you were not allowed to utter a word. Anyone who talked to you would be at risk of the same punishment, so essentially you were shamed and ostracized by your own community.

There were caravans at the back of large grounds where those *bad people* would go and stay in isolation as if their very thoughts were contagious and could infect us all. My peers were sent off to programmes to re-program their thinking if they were asking the wrong kinds of questions and there were times people simply were disappeared – not in a murderous way but they were kicked out of the group and made to fend for themselves, not to be heard of again.

While there were amazing elements to commune life there was the continuous undercurrent that this was a war mission. This was serious. We were groomed to be what they called 'God's Endtime Army' from birth. Teenage angst had another layer to it. It wasn't just 'Who am I?',

'Will anyone find me attractive?', 'Who should I be in this world?' Instead, it was 'Are you fitting in and if not, what is wrong with you?', 'Exorcise thyself, work, sacrifice, try harder, hide the unaligned bits of yourself and become *WHO YOU'RE SUPPOSED TO BE!*'

While I was still on my tedious kitchen duties, a travelling group of young people visited from their mission in Russia and led that evening's devotional gathering. They put out a call to action for anyone willing to join them and I knew this was my chance. I remember writing them a highly persuasive letter after they'd left to go back to the field, obsessing about whether they would respond, hoping this could be my way out. I remember saying something clever in the letter like 'Is your invitation to join just a political ploy or are you serious? Because I'm ready to take you up on your offer.' I told myself that this persuasive sentence cornered them, leading them to discuss at length whether they had room for me (maybe they even prayed about it) and agreed that they couldn't say no because of that sentence. This was my first evidence of the power of my own words and I would fantasize at length about being a writer, and using the power of persuasion through the written word.

Nobody ever asked me what I wanted to be when I grew up.

Growing up wasn't an option here.

It would be self-indulgent to assume otherwise.

I now realize that those of you who have been asked 'What do you want to be when you grow up?' countless times from the age of three years old wear a different kind of shackle. You experienced the pressure to decide what future was possible for someone like you, with your specific intellect, skills, work ethic and family expectations. You then carried that right through the pressured education system, which tried to mould you into a good factory worker or employee – into someone who fits into a schedule, says yes, has limited original thought and is kept on a path of 'shoulds'.

There was a theme to my therapy clients when I had an active private practice. Mostly women, but some men, in their early 30s who arguably had good lives, jobs and support networks – but who were anxious or depressed, saying that their expectations (or rather the ones put on them by society) had not played out yet and therefore they were melancholic with feelings of being failures, lost in society with questions about everything.

Over time, I slowly built evidence that I wasn't the only one who struggled mentally based on expectations thrust upon me. Even though my experience was on the extreme end of the life continuum, this was a challenge across society.

It has become a popular notion that, if you haven't achieved what you expected of yourself, based on what society and your cultural lens told you was possible, then you have full right to judge yourself as a failure. I've seen that it's this mismatch between what your life has become and your expectation that leads to a variety of symptoms such as anxious thinking, depressive episodes or physical health issues to name a few.

Eventually, I got a reply from the front-line mission!

I would need to prepare, I would need to bring money but I could come to Russia for six months and we could see how it went.

I can still say, to this day, that this became one of the most adventurous years of my life! I remember visiting my parents before leaving, preparing for the harsh winter, for travel and fully living the dream I always held on to.

Flying to Moscow, meeting a stranger who was part of the group and getting on a 22-hour sleeper train to the heart of the Ural Mountains was nothing I'd ever done alone before. My eyes were wide open, this felt right, like it was leading me to my mission. I was meant for something more. I was special and this would be my path to proving it.

During that coming-of-age year I tried proper alcohol for the first time. An awkward shy teenager who never fully fitted in, alcohol opened a totally new world of possibility.

The first time I had a drink, I remember the whoosh at the back of my brain, my shoulders fell back just a little and confidence coursed through my soul. I suddenly knew who I was and felt the power of me, it was like I could look at the world through new eyes and everything made sense. I danced free, I flirted, I was particularly hilarious and laughed with my whole body when others made jokes. I now realize I probably had low-level anxiety my whole life and suddenly all of this tension went away – a bridge to another me, someone I could get on board with.

Writing these tales from my own experiences and struggles with mental health cause flashes of memory to swish through me. Why was I anxious? Why couldn't I tell anyone? Why did I not just feel normal?

There was a time when I was younger when a dozen of us were illegally in the back of a van with no windows, driving across a European border, told to be quiet while papers were asked for and we were meant to pray that the *wolves* didn't take us *sheep*. It was always an 'us versus them' feeling – the Lord would protect us (which should have reduced anxiety) but sometimes he wouldn't, for reasons we would discover later (God had to teach that person a lesson, there was darkness in their heart, etc). So many unknowns, so many surprises. I needed to remain alert.

I was welcomed in the home in Russia to a totally different vibe from the giant 80-person home I'd been in. This was a mission in the field doing real work, not just talking about it. Everyone was young – maybe the oldest was 25 – there must have been 15 of us in two cosy apartments in the heart of the city

There was also vodka. The clear liquid of pure freedom. I would come of age here, experiencing excitement, purpose, danger and finding just a little more of myself. I saw real problems, homelessness, parentless children, drug problems, sickness, poverty and the biggest smiles I'd ever seen. We didn't have problems in our communes; we were part of the solution.

We ran an amazing project with the kids, which I truly believe was impactful and helped change lives. We worked alongside the government, found sponsors, and this project is still going to this day run by the local Russian people. We also had a project in prisons where we would sing to the inmates and try to save their souls. These weren't just any prisons; these were off the back of the Gulag heritage and many of them were completely inaccessible in the winter. It was an epic summer; we drove miles of wastelands with generals and soldier friends who escorted us to prisons with triple security measures and stages where we would sing and make these men very happy. At the time I didn't find this all that seedy and some people genuinely loved the music and the company but now, looking back at pictures, I was so young, innocent and beautiful, and I didn't know the difference between genuine interest and being taken advantage of in an abusive way.

When I left two winters later I felt bonded to my team for life. Bonded through booze, trauma, adventure and experience. I was sad to go but also felt I simply couldn't stay there forever; I was on a journey of discovery, which had to continue.

When I got back to Belgium I was lost. Back to just my family and one other family down the road, I was back to trying to fit in while being completely different from everyone else. My parents were still leaders even though everything was disparate and pointless. I was by default a leaders' daughter and that held certain responsibilities. I'd seen the world and couldn't see what was around me in the same way as before. Maybe I was arrogant, as many 18-year-olds are, but I knew in my heart that I knew better than these idiots.

This is where I began my double life.

Being seen as my whole true self would be dangerous so I began to craft two versions of me – one was the leaders' daughter, who said the right things and showed up in the right way while the other version hid and cried, drank and played, was hedonistic and troubled, trying to understand how everything I'd been taught my whole life married up with what I had now experienced. Who am I? Where am I supposed to be?

Wearing a mask is an interesting thing. So many of us do it and I believe it's a seed that can grow into mental health issues over time. The squashing of feelings, repressing of thoughts, morphing into someone expected and hiding your true self. Over time your real identity becomes so small, contorted and twisted that you can't even hear them properly or know what they have to say. It's just like in the movie *Get Out* (2017), where the characters' true consciousness is locked away in the sunken place and replaced by a false identity. You're there but you're not there.

I never knew what real affection or attention meant, I didn't know the difference between kindness and abuse. I'd never had attention focused on me just for being me, I was always someone's side interest, never worthy of actual love. I was a side-thing, a curiosity, someone whose blonde hair got touched and whose body was gawped at. I wanted so much to be loved for my mind, for my ambition, for who I was and yet nobody saw any of that – it almost convinced me that there wasn't any of that there and being loved for being me was just a lost hope – so I got what I could get – even if it meant total abuse along the way.

The threat of God rescinding his blessings was real and powerful. I would be warned that people on the outside were evil, while also being trained to entertain and be open with those on the inside. I was told that sex was a tool for salvation and, while it was permissible to say no, it was not advisable.

Legends were told of those from my generation who would leave and go out into the lecherous world and turn into prostitutes or drug addicts and become homeless. This was a lesson of the evil that was in the world and how we wouldn't be in a safe haven of protection if we decided to leave. When things went well it was all credit to the group; when they went wrong all the blame was on us.

I've since seen this environment recreated in corporations globally. Finding the scapegoat when something goes wrong but, when something goes right, 'We're all in this together'. The belief systems that just are because they always have been, if you question them you're seen as a difficult, a troublemaker and eventually get disappeared (usually fired in this context).

A double life becomes essential for survival: you show up exactly as they want you to be – a clone of their words, values, dress sense and habits. Talk lightly about your family or hobbies so that you seem like a real person, just enough so that you are not forgettable, laugh at the pub, buy a round of drinks, but never, never let the mask slip.

Now you may be thinking it's not like that any more, that the world is changing, people are opening up, the younger generation are showing up differently – and while, yes, there is plenty of progress, I'm seeing that the masks are just evolving into something different. These days people talk about their busyness, side hustles, achievements, holidays, followers and maybe dating or property prices. They tell stories that feel real but on the inside we are playing a game of *should* and just longing for connection. We're lonelier than ever and our mental health is worse than it ever was and we pretend with more and more energy to be someone we think is most likely to fit in, get paid and survive. I will explore the many reasons for this in the chapters to come but one of the key reasons is the fear we have about removing our masks and the lack of safety we feel about being our true selves – especially in the workplace!

So my mask wearing started early, before I knew any better. I just wanted to feel normal, so I pretended to fit in while the pressure built and built until I couldn't stand any more.

When I was 18, my stepfather decided to leave my mother. She was in shock – never having paid a bill in her adult life or run a household on her own. While she was still a leader and felt a clear calling to continue in her mission she would veer in and out of undiagnosed depression, trying to hold on to her purpose and her mask – I wonder still if she ever told anyone what she was going through or, like a true shepherd (our word for leader), she just kept smiling and praying, hoping that she would still be trusted in her role. I spent some time driving her around Europe visiting homes – I would comfort her by wearing my mask too.

When I returned, I would see my sister who'd already left the group and was attempting to study and build up the pieces of a *normal* life. This was my exit strategy – a place to forget, to find myself, to wonder at everything – here began my second life, hedonistic, risk taking, wild, filled with that sweet nectar of peace – alcohol.

I partied hard, drank to oblivion, stacked up shameful stories and kept drinking in order not to think. These stories started as the kind of silliness I imagine all teenagers experience when they're finding themselves – losing things, staying up all night, flirty encounters, hilarious tales to be laughed about the next day. They developed into regular blackouts, drug taking without much thought for what I was doing, getting separated from who I was with, finding myself in strange beds, losing my shoes, getting arrested, getting pushed around by scary people, finding myself in dangerous crowds, having unsafe sex and waking up the next day to assess the bruises and pick up the pieces.

I didn't know if this was still fun but I didn't know who else to be. While there were definitely a list of traumas stacking on top of each other throughout my life, on one particular night a new trauma would sear into my brain and develop into the PTSD that I still deal with today.

This section holds a trigger warning for anyone who has ever been assaulted or holds on to the trauma that can come from being a woman in a man's world. I've questioned whether I should tell this part of the story, but it explains where my mental health got to and maybe it will give you an angle on your story too.

One night, after I had been out with my friends, I ended up in a stranger's flat. That night I was repeatedly raped while I zoned in and out of blackout. I tried to grab my senses, looked for exits through the haze and, as dawn broke, I finally found a door that would lead me to open air. I didn't know where I was so I walked for what seemed like hours to find my way home.

Everything had changed and yet nothing had. I remember arriving finally at my mother's flat where some of my sisters were and everyone greeted me like normal. Inside I was shouting for someone to see me, to notice that everything had changed, to look after me like the helpless girl I was and yet my mask-wearing skills were so sharp that no one could see what I really wanted to say.

While today I'm diagnosed with complex PTSD, it was this incident that would stay seared in my mind for decades. I would see the perpetrator's face in crowds, I would flash back in random situations, it would affect later relationships and would mostly make me hate myself. After all, I had been drinking and had gotten myself into this situation, so it must have been my fault. Society is set up to make it the victim's fault and, given my state of mind, I wouldn't have been able to ID him properly, so it didn't even cross my mind to try to report him. My memory was hazy, I had been stupid and put myself into a dangerous situation. As my upbringing had taught me, if something bad happened then it must have been my fault – this was God's punishment for veering off his path.

It's taken me many years to truly understand that even if a woman is in a vulnerable state, that still under no circumstance is it right or OK for someone to violate us, abuse or rape us. And so, please if you're the person who needs to read this – it's not your fault. You are loveable. You are enough!

Before, I had been drinking to find myself but now I wanted to hurt myself. To absolve the shame and horror that had poisoned my blood, to get rid of the awfulness that was me. While my brain now knows that I am not to blame, my shame response often does not. I still feel the blame of my actions in my body and I still try to run away from how this makes me feel.

I've realized since, in my work with young people and extensive work in the mental health space, that people generally aren't angry for no reason. People aren't mean on purpose, there's usually a deep pain that cannot be spoken, a hurt that overwhelms their soul, and yes, while we can learn to emotionally regulate, what we also do is learn to lock away our pain. We bury it so far down that we think it can't be found but eventually, over time, it seeps up through the cracks – it leaks in a variety of ways, which include anger, but also include anxiety, depression and a whole host of other mental or physical health challenges.

When we keep things buried and repressed these often-valid feelings show up in other ways. I would keep things buried for a very long time – but that didn't mean these things went away – they just waited.

I then went to Africa for eight months to live alongside my brother and his team. There were strict routines and rules, including very limited access to finance or booze but access to beautiful beaches and a place to breathe. While this mostly acted as respite, there was a strange couple in charge of things who were nice if you did what they wanted but would flip if you had a voice or did something else. I was asked for free sex by people much older than me and found it within myself to refuse. I questioned things and clashed with those in charge, beginning to wonder why some people had all the power and why we blindly agreed without any questions.

When I returned to Europe I would pick up my double life again, eventually dating (or should I say regularly partying) with someone outside of the cult, which was strictly against the rules of the game. While you may be picturing a sad, traumatized, angry young adult, make no mistake that's not what other people saw – on these pages I can tell you what my internal world felt like back then but remember the mask? I was highly trusted and with a new restructure across Europe, I was now leading on boards and would get my travel costs covered so I could attend meetings, take part in gatherings and be part of something. I had learnt to be persuasive when I spoke and had built a decent reputation for myself – people knew who I was and I had built just a little bit of cool within my personal brand. Slaving in kitchens was well behind me and I had channelled my powers of persuasion to fit into this place.

The temptation for a double life was strong now that I was back. So many of our generation had left the group, were trying other lifestyles and yet I held on to the one place where I was slightly seen. What was I going to do on the outside? I had no education, no way to really make money and would be as invisible as I had been my whole childhood. I was afraid too – my PTSD was beginning to lock in and so I rationalized the belief system so that it could override all the questions I had about abuses of power and what I now know eventually led me into a position of experiencing assault. I told myself that what we believed was pure but people somehow got it wrong – including me!

I was connected to the heart of our purpose and turned a blind eye to the long list of things that were wrong. I looked back for the longest time and judged myself for not being brave enough to leave, to stand up. My notoriety, my idealism and ambition blinded me to the reality of trauma locking in all around us. Every time a question or doubt showed up I just fortified myself against it. Reading about other places in library books, drinking to laugh and forget, hating myself secretly while enjoying the small opportunities where I would be seen and noticed.

At 22 I became pregnant and my illicit affair became public. This meant I would either have to be demoted and prove my worth within the group or it could be a catalyst to change things. I was tired and lost and rationalized that God would want my son to have a father and perhaps I was doing the right thing by prioritizing my child. The father of my child was a good man and immediately invited me to live with him in London. This would be the break from everything from my past and give me a possibility at a future.

People often ask me when I speak on stage 'How did you escape?' They imagine walls and maybe even guns, physical things to keep you in. What they don't realize is that in these situations none of those things exist, the walls are not physical, the weapons are not pointed at you, what happens over time is that the real walls form in your mind. I often think of the movie *The Shawshank Redemption*, where it takes years of digging through the wall and a final night of intense planning, crawling through and finally falling into sewer water to stand up in the rain, hands aloft, finally a free man. I wish that was the end of my story, that being washed in the rain was the end of one life and the beginning of a blissful new one. That being rescued by a handsome prince and given a family of my own would be the happy ending and life would be simple from there.

But instead, there are no walls. You are told you're free the whole time so there's nothing to escape as far as you're concerned. None of it makes sense, it isn't a linear path like digging a hole through a tunnel with a spoon. Instead, after being institutionalized, the slow torture of freedom is a much greater burden than the safety of a clear belief system, community and routine. Now that I was safe, I would begin to feel. I would begin to feel betrayed, lied to and unsure of how to live in this world, a world that was always pitched as a bad, scary place.

Having grown up around people my whole life, the experience of not knowing anyone except my boyfriend (who was away at work for eight hours a day) was the loneliest time of my life. I even pushed away those I did know in an effort to finally discover whether it was actually possible to think for myself.

There's nothing like alone time to force you to confront yourself, to question your thinking and to wonder if anything actually matters. I was back to being invisible, stripped of any achievement I'd ever made, trying desperately to grasp a new mask that would work in this weird world. I still had thoughts about God having a plan; this was leading me somewhere – like the biblical character Job who was tested, stayed strong and then got through – this was my test. I didn't understand where it would take me but one thing I did know – I was made for more.

Since I didn't know what normal was I was trying my best to adapt into my boyfriend's family, their unspoken rules and norms, which over time eroded my sense of self further. I will always be grateful to my now ex-husband and his family for the patience and care they showed me over the years – and yet at the time I tried morphing into how they saw the world which wasn't my true self either and perpetuated my depression and addictions.

Was everything I knew a lie? I didn't have an education so due to sheer frustration I started a college counselling course one day a week and other than that poured as much of my energy into my son as I could. In 2005 I was pregnant with my daughter, which was when the next significant event would show up – it was all over the news and I was alone in defending and explaining my past.

Ricky Rodriguez, the son of the founder, had intended to murder his mother (who was then the leader of the cult) but she had sent a previous nanny of his instead to have the conversation he was after. He would go on to murder his nanny and take his own life. He posted a suicide note in the form of a video online, which would be a large part of a documentary made about his story. This video was a letter to us, his peers, explaining the immense pressure he was under to save us, the abuse he'd endured, the propaganda that had his face all over it and that he was doing this for us. The senior leaders had always been in hiding, escaping the law while the smaller homes went through pre-dawn raids and court cases. They lived on our tithe money and were always just out of reach. Ricky was trying to save us in the only way that was left to him. He spoke of my generation's pain and confusion and took the law into his own hands. This was the most public display of our pain that I had ever seen; my boyfriend said I had to watch it, and he asked me what I thought.

I didn't know what to think. I was angry but I didn't understand why. Hadn't I had a good experience? Wasn't the mission good? I didn't know what to believe any more.

Soon after, I heard of the explanations that came from the group (now known as The Family), including letters by his mother Maria Zerby, which gave the reasons for her son's suicide from her perspective – his own mother! She explained that he had been a beautiful boy but had been taken to the dark side through his doubt and disbelief. This included a threat: let this be a warning to any of us who were doubting, as this is where our own actions would lead. She took no responsibility.

There are clear parallels in the corporate world. When an employee is burnt out, depressed, addicted or suicidal, it is often put down to chemical imbalances and the individual's responsibility – it's considered their sole responsibility to get help. Simply offering a mental health benefit seems to be all the responsibility the organization will take. When the employee who is struggling asks for help, leaders, managers and HR often get nervous, highlighting how only professionals can 'handle' these conversations and so they quickly outsource to helplines, self-help apps or other external health services. Rarely do employers have clear and open conversations, ask direct questions about mental health and look at their systems, their working practices, their policies and misuses of power as having any impact on the mental health of their employees.

Having said that, what I hear all the time is that when someone takes their life, rarely do the people around them know they were even struggling. Sometimes their mask was fixed on so perfectly that they may have been heralded as the life and soul of the party or the person that other people turned to for advice. Our current approach to mental health focuses so heavily on the risk factors, the signs and the symptoms but, by the time that these are visible, it's often too late.

Why aren't we focused on creating healthy environments, honest spaces and normalized conversations for everyone about everything, giving opportunities to remove the mask long before the cracks are showing and before it gets messy and ugly? Depression is an internal struggle but a collective responsibility and we desperately need to question our wider responsibilities within our organizations and society at large.

My daughter was born in 2006 and while I experienced post-natal depression with both of my children, my alcohol addiction would get out of control this time. My thoughts got darker, I felt angrier and began hiding alcohol, becoming a shadow of myself and I drank to harm myself rather than just escape. I put myself in danger many times, driving while blackout drunk and I hesitate to admit in writing the number of times I put my kids in danger.

I would wake up with my clothes ripped and my mouth dry – fresh from blackout, panicked thoughts wondering if my kids were still here, checking where my car was and, more often than not, checking the bonnet for stains or dents that would help me piece together the night before. I was angry and I took it out on my partner. On the outside we had a good life: a house, two healthy kids, a car and enough money to live – I was still studying to be a counsellor too – but on the inside poison was spreading and my pain was all consuming. The shame stacked and stacked, I remember trying to collect myself in the college bathroom, vomiting at my kids' playgroups, disappearing when I didn't have them without language to explain what was going on.

Everything I'd ever known was a lie. Everything I knew about myself, worked towards, believed and fought for was wrong. Everyone I'd loved and trusted had lied to me. I'd put myself in repeated abusive situations to the point of rape and violence because I'd never been taught boundaries or self-respect. I'd never invested in my future because I didn't think there was a future to invest in. I was now stuck on this earth for a lifetime, with two kids, and I was trapped in an endless loop of responsibility without having learnt any responsibility for myself. I was bred to be special, told from birth that I wasn't just anybody but that I was *some-body* and now, look what I'd done. I still internalized that I was a bad person because of how my life turned out, a filthy drunk, an abusive perpetrator repeating cycles of trauma with barely any education or hope for any life ahead of me. I was 26 and had no hope, no prospects and had convinced myself that my own kids would be better off without me.

I'd thought of taking my life many times. When driving I would want to swerve off a bridge or into a concrete wall. I would weigh up whether to take them with me or do this alone, what would be better for them, what would be better for everyone.

People often call the person who's died by suicide selfish – but what they don't understand is that when you're in that all-consuming horrific mindset, your brain tells you that it's the most selfless thing you can do. That you're saving others, that you're a burden and, while people aren't saying it aloud, you've convinced yourself they're thinking it.

One morning at 6 am, I remember staring at my ceiling and thinking 'I cannot do another day. I cannot get through the next hour much less the rest of the day. My body won't move, my brain cannot hold space, this is it'.

And for some reason, soon after another thought floated into my mind. Now let me be clear, this is not professional advice, that will come later, this is simply my story and what happened to me.

The second thought was 'What if I postponed taking my life for one year?'

I would have nothing left to lose, I would have my exit strategy and this would free me up. It would leave me free to experiment with all the self-help and well-being tools that were out there. I didn't believe any of them would work for me but what difference would a year make if I was confident I could leave this way eventually?

People like to think that recovery is linear. That we make decisions and then everything falls into place. The reality is that recovery is messy, it's stop-start, it's learning on the job and pivoting as you go.

That year came and went, and life wasn't perfect, but I learnt a few things that would act as principles for the rest of my life. I learnt that we can teach ourselves to be happy! That well-being isn't a one size fits all, it is a personal journey of agency, experimenting and self-awareness and just taking one step at a time can lead to greatness.

I had to start with putting down the booze – completely. When I was 29 I went to Alcoholics Anonymous (AA) for several life-saving years. I rarely go now because while they start by giving you a structure for sobriety they eventually risk taking your agency away – but what they gave me was a lesson in honesty and community.

I observed people being radically honest about themselves and their own behaviour and this was a revelation to me. People could actually say exactly what they thought and others would listen to them and offer hugs, this was incredible to me. I don't think I'd ever seen anyone be truly honest about themselves, mess and all. This was different from the godly confessions that I was coerced to make in my childhood – this was actual real talk!

My first forays into honesty were a royal mess. Short bursts of sentences amidst snot, tears and shaking. I would need lots of practice to get better at this.

Other things I experimented with… I'd listen to a three-minute guided meditation to help with emotional regulation. When you have numbed yourself for so long through drinking or another avenue, to actually *feel* becomes an overwhelming and sometimes traumatizing experience. To feel when you have squashed down feelings for so long is like an assault on the body. Tears roll down your face, anxiety courses through your body, and shame arises as you notice your part in other people's pain.

I had to sit with the knowledge that I had been a terrible parent. A perpetrator of hot–cold behaviour, my PTSD making me jumpy, shouty, mean. I was that person. I began to realize that I couldn't use my past victimhood forever as my children wouldn't see it that way. Regardless of my reasons, my anger, my past, I was now continuing the cycle of generational trauma. I had done this. This was on me. And so I had to find a way to change. It didn't matter that this was inflicted upon me by people in my past – that would only keep me stuck – I had to take radical responsibility for my mental health.

I used the mantra from AA long after I stopped going. It's dog-eared and sits in an old wallet as, whenever my negative impulses returned, I would pick it up and read:

> Just for today I will try to live through this day only and not tackle my whole life problem at once.

Just for today I will be happy. Most folks are as happy as they make up their minds to be. (Alcoholics Anonymous, 1921)

Could we really decide to be happy? This didn't make any sense to me at the time. I simply held on to this paper with tears in my eyes, wondering how I would ever make anything of the mess I'd become.

Would I ever make a mark in the world, find a career, repair the damage I'd made, live with my trauma? There were too many questions and all I had to do for now was show up, survive, keep it simple, be honest, do the work.

People didn't realize what was going on behind the scenes while I studied part time to be a counsellor (I realize the irony!).

I practised slowly being more of myself at college too. I remember one of the first lessons when my alcohol addiction was rife. We were introducing ourselves in our second year and our tutor asked us to tell the group something about ourselves. I froze with panicked thoughts wondering what version of the truth I would share – I would need to live with whatever I said that day for the next year at least. I suppose the tutor could recognize weakness as she asked me to go first. I burst into tears.

I told a version of the truth: the one that makes people's ears perk up but doesn't cause their faces to twist into that uncomfortable curiosity I've seen so often (even in therapists). I see how they change the way they see me. Now I am not a person but a curiosity, a case study – entertainment. I know when to play this up or play this down depending on my state of mind, and if I want to see people again or if I'll drop them like I have so many others.

People think that the hardest thing about addiction is giving up the substance but it isn't – it's living with what you've done and who you are. It's facing up every day, not through big sweeping statements or gestures, but through the small daily practices that create a lifetime of change.

So what was the transition from this snail-like pace of survival into the person I am today? And what does this have to do with work, your success and the global mental health crisis?

I believe work can be one of the best *protective factors* that we have when done right. That means work can be good for our mental health, something that gives us routine, purpose, community, fulfilment and skills development, which are well-known pillars for overall well-being.

The 'five ways to well-being' researched by the New Economics Foundation (Aked et al, 2008) list these five ways as key to our overall well-being: Connect, Be active, Take notice, Keep learning, Give. Now if these can be provided to you each day during your working hours, then your mental well-being will be so much better than when you use the hours outside of work to mentally prepare yourself for its difficulties.

Two years after I got sober I got my first full-time job. My counselling qualification allowed me to be a keyworker for a youth charity. I would mentor and support young people to live better lives. This would help me learn that everyone had a story and, while my story was somewhat unique, there were stories that were much worse than mine. I realize that there were people out there beyond my self-obsessed survival ego, that there were plenty of versions of my story: people who had experienced trauma, were battling with their own mental health, were making the choice about whether to be a victim or not and were trying to make their way in the world.

This is where I would meet George – a 16-year-old self-proclaimed white supremacist who was really a traumatized boy with a dying mother who wanted a tribe.

It's also where I would meet Diante, a gang member who was just trying to be someone, trying to matter in the world. It's where I found a routine and learnt from probably the best leadership I've seen in my career.

I will always remember how my manager, Phil Walters, would find the time for me no matter what stress he had going on. I would ask stupid questions, I wanted to do well but I had never really held a proper job in my life. I'd somehow sold myself in the interview and, looking back, I didn't really know anything about what people did at work. Yet he slowed down, listened, advised and supported me whenever I needed it.

A year later I thought it would be great to get a degree – and why get a bachelor's degree if there was a way to skip this step and get a Master's. This is one of those far-away concepts that I thought would never ever be possible for someone like me. I'd never learnt that fundamental task of how to learn. How to work to an exam, how to give the tutor what they want to hear in order to pass.

I didn't know much, which meant that I didn't know what was impossible either, so I would try any opportunity. I decided to apply for a part-time MSc programme at Birkbeck in London. I didn't know how I would afford to pay for it or how I would manage with a full-time job, two growing kids and my tenuous sobriety and mental health but I went ahead and applied.

My naïveté stood me in good stead. Even though I was sure I wouldn't get in, I told myself that I had nothing to lose and tried anyway.

When I received an invitation for an interview, my body was overwhelmed at simply being given the opportunity to try. I'd read books about this in the library – people who had nothing and came back from the brink of death or trauma to study and go on to have actual careers. They were my silent mentors and inspiration.

I was fascinated by the idea of having a career, becoming an intelligent person and had no idea how to really feel about the world of work.

When I walk across London Bridge into the city – even today – it actually fills me with joy! I think of being part of the wonderful, beautiful rat race – what a privilege to wake up every day and be able to work! It's funny how our conditioning and perspective can change our view of things – for some people the rat race captures a necessary horror to become successful; for me, it's always been a privilege – to be alive, to be able to work and engage with society!

When I was invited to interview I was nervous – what version of the truth would give me just enough edge to be memorable but not too much for them to judge me a liability. One thing I'd gotten good at was spin. I'd learnt it through selling the dream my whole childhood straight through to the masks I'd worn to survive. I told some truth about my alternative past, how important education was to me and how hard I would work.

I was accepted.

The next two years would be hard because of the mental stamina and sheer determination it would take. I'd never worked harder to intentionally take responsibility for my life and change it.

Now at least I was headed somewhere. Towards the end of my degree, I would wake up at 3 am to study before my kids woke up and I would go to work. I would visualize the end game long before I knew the buzzword of visualization. I powered through this period by picturing the end result in my mind countless times. So by the time I walked up on the stage in a cap and gown to receive my degree, I had done it a million times before.

I would go on to work in the charity sector for some time. Youth work, youth mental health and eventually move into corporate mental health as clinical director for an EAP (employee assistance programme). I would become frustrated and restless, continuing to work on my skills and get better, excited to be advising organizations on how to challenge stigma and focus on mental health but frustrated that the very places that were advising on change were often toxic and dysfunctional themselves.

Having grown up in a toxic environment and having worked relentlessly on my sobriety and mental health, I struggled to deal with my hypocrisy and working in toxic environments. My mental health was too important. As long as I had some agency and autonomy in my role I would stay, and when that ran out I would leave.

There was one job that I left within three months because it was so toxic that I knew the pay cheque was not worth sacrificing my mental well-being. This can occur in any position – these were roles that were supposed to be purposeful and supportive. While this is a privileged option that isn't always available, I do urge you to reflect and ask yourself whether you're overlooking your mental health for salary or status and at what cost in the long run.

My mental health is a lifelong journey, which I have to manage. I live with PTSD and still have times of total frustration when I'm in pain and want to solve or heal it but I've learnt that the goal isn't to fix myself. Those of us who experience mental illness are not broken, we have access to an opportunity to see the world differently and to learn great things. I've learnt to change my perspective from one of a clear destination and goal (which is how society sets us up to think about success) to one that is circular, a journey where things happen along the way and sometimes my trauma gets the better of me and that's OK.

What people don't realize is that those of us with these challenges will sometimes be the most ambitious, hardworking and passionate people you'll ever meet. We're an asset at work because not only have we built careers, we've also survived staring into the abyss, built resilience through pain, are adaptable in struggle and, when the tough times happen, we are strong and unfazed. When the pandemic hit, my body was calm as I'd been preparing for the end of the world my whole life. Bring. It. On.

Not many people can say the same.

Sometimes I still think I give my thoughts away to the highest bidder. We all do. Someone else's idea of what success should look like for me, someone else's idea of how I should treat my symptoms, invest in myself, or even the path I should take – buy a house, get married, raise children in a system that limits their ability to think for themselves – and slowly my body feels more sluggish, my frustration mounts, I have more mental health challenges and my relationships suffer.

And I have to catch myself. I have to take a step back and ask myself a few questions: Why am I this frustrated when I really have a good life? Why is there friction in my relationships? Why am I getting more headaches? Why is my PTSD flaring up more?

In his book *Solve for Happy* (2017), Mo Gawdat describes his happiness equation: 'your happiness' he says, 'is equal to or greater than the difference between the events of your life and your expectations of how life should behave.'

When society, media and culture are telling us that our expectations should be one thing when we actually want something else, no wonder we're more depressed than ever!

In order to be happier we may need to think about our expectations differently. We can still be ambitious and we can still work hard to achieve what we want, but we need to start thinking for ourselves and aligning our expectations to what we actually want. Then we'll have more opportunities to experience happiness.

So enough about me. Suffice it to say that my life experience and subsequent studies have made me look hard at the topic of mental health, culture and society, first as a way for me to be free and then subsequently to see how life could be better for others.

I got divorced in 2016 and, while it seems sad, this decision and action was one of my first true independent thoughts. It felt visceral, like finally being brave enough to leave the cult, to do something that my body and mind said would be good for me.

I left a good job in 2017 and set out on my own not because I had a perfect plan or even knew where I would get to – I just knew what I didn't want. I didn't want to live anyone else's version of my life any more and so I stepped out into the unknown – the unknown that would lead to building a business, finding myself, finding love, speaking on global stages, building my kids' ability to think for themselves, feeling excitement at being alive and not ever experiencing depression again.

The next chapter is about you. What success means to you, what your body may be telling you and why we're getting the mental health narrative at work so wrong in so many ways. The next chapters are about hope, that if we can see where we've gotten stuck living someone else's narrative of our lives we might just be able to press pause on things, turn the rudder on the ship, go in the direction we were meant for and thereby reduce some of the symptoms we keep trying to solve.

CHAPTER TWO

Why you?

What does success mean to you?

The Cambridge Dictionary (nd) defines success as 'the achieving of results wanted or hoped for' or 'something that achieves positive results'.

Society has added plenty of subjective ideas to what those *results* should be connected to – money, status or fame to name a few.

But what if we also look at success as achieving a mentally healthy state of mind, contentment, optimal health, relationships that help us thrive, raising children who can think for themselves or achieving the result of going a completely different way? Whether that's living on a boat, climbing a mountain, experiencing love, seeing new things, being an entrepreneur... the list could go on.

When we're at work we're often in that boiled frog scenario. You know the story – the frog dips its toe in a boiling pot and jumps the hell out of there – it's toxic and will likely kill him quickly – he's having none of it! But if the frog dives into the pot while it's still cool, the temperature change is so incremental that he doesn't realize that he's slowly being boiled to death in that same toxicity – it just has a gradual onset.

We don't go to an interview and say 'man this place is toxic, I'm jumping right in!' Instead we hear the best-case scenario, the benefits, the possibilities and of course the salary and progression route that will lead to our idea of *success* and then we start swimming. It's over time that the messages sour, management show their true colours, we hit a cap on our free thinking, we see things that go against our values, etc. But by that point we've sold ourselves the dream in our head: we enjoy the salary, we like the illusion of safety, there are some good things we get to do, we want to be successful and so we stay until we slowly start to boil.

We don't realize what's happening until we start feeling that things are off and even then we ignore it for as long as possible. Surely no one would intentionally boil me, that would be ridiculous, surely it's a me-problem. I'll just work harder, wake up earlier, exercise harder, listen to more podcasts, hustle more, meditate better, schedule my time more efficiently and eventually I'll get it.

Until you don't.

Your sleep suffers, your relationships become tense, your body starts to ache and an emptiness floats in. I'll talk about what all this could mean and what to do about it in later chapters but this chapter is for you if you've felt any of these things. Burnout, anxiety, depression, that flat empty feeling, that frustration at not having *made it*. Maybe you've achieved success at work but you're lonely and flat at home, maybe you're winning as far as wealth and notoriety but wondering why it doesn't feel like you thought it would. The hamster wheel just gets faster as you try to sustain the success level you've achieved.

The question I want to pose is this: what if work was good for your health, not just something you have to recover from later?

How many times have you put up, shut up or soldiered on at work? Skipped your lunch break, come in early, stayed late, worked on the weekends or during your holiday? You usually pay the price for it later – probably alone or in your therapist's or doctor's office. You've spent your weekends sleeping or so zoned out that there was barely any energy for a social life other than drinking to forget or convincing yourself that this is normal and that you should keep grinding.

Maybe you're even trying to be the change at work (which I think is wonderful and I will give you some tools for how to do this better later in this book!), maybe you're part of a network, a mental health ambassador group, you're challenging stigma, a diversity and inclusion ally, LGBTQI+ or gender issues advocate, and you've been excited to have a voice and create real change.

But over time the group doesn't seem to be making the change you'd hoped for. Morale is low, your meetings are about the next awareness initiative you want to run and in the end, you don't have the time. You're stressed and

thought you would be part of something inspiring, a movement for change, rather than just adding even more things
to your never-ending to-do list.

Maybe you're from one of the minority groups that is
consistently experiencing micro-aggressions or maybe
you're being micromanaged in a hybrid workplace. Maybe
you're a junior employee who is being abused by your
managers and maybe you've even been seeing a therapist
or business coach but everything is perpetuating the same
ideas: just get your time management and goals right, work
a little bit harder and one day you'll reach the elusive place
where everything will be OK. Where it will be easier, where
your relationships will thrive and you'll have achieved that
ultimate goal: success.

If you're feeling a sense of emptiness… you are not alone.

If you feel like everything is working on a knife's edge,
that you just have to keep moving forward or everything
will fall apart… you are not alone.

If you feel like you've achieved success but it doesn't feel
like you thought it should… you are not alone.

If you feel like you're on a path that's been set for you
by parents, teachers, friends, society, religion or other influences in your life when you don't even know what you
want… you are not alone.

If you've done everything right and according to the
rule book but there's this gnawing feeling in your gut that
you just don't like any of it… you are not alone.

If you're tired and feeling the strain on your body or
your mental health… you are not alone.

If you are experiencing a crisis because you've been
diagnosed with burnout, illness, anxiety, depression or

have been feeling suicidal and think there's no point… you are not alone.

If you feel like the workplace has to change, your version of success has to change and there's only so much you can do before we have to also question the overall system and how our thoughts are influenced… you are not alone.

In these next pages I want to show you some questions to ask yourself. Some ideas for how to approach things differently in your life and how collectively, if we all think differently, maybe we can change the systems around us as well.

Why the current approach to well-being at work is wrong!

As a therapist, I've spoken to employees for years about their mental health. Having been the clinical director for an employee assistance programme, I also know on the back end what support there is on offer for employees. As CEO and founder of PVL I've worked with global organizations, helping them work out the gaps in their well-being offerings, and crucially, helping them change their approach to one that is striving for a mentally healthy organization rather than merely putting benefits in place for people who are actively struggling.

There are a few things we're getting wrong:

- How we define mental health
- Outsourcing the *problem* to helplines and benefits (and our language when pointing to these services)

- Our over-reliance on technology as a solution
- Old-school therapies that need updating to support people differently in a rapidly changing world
- Our sole focus on the individual when there is a wider system and culture to think about

How we define mental health and the trouble with benefits

Mental health is about all of us – it's about the health of our mind.

The World Health Organization (2014) defines mental health as a 'state of well-being in which every individual realizes his or her own potential, can cope with the normal stresses of life, can work productively and fruitfully, and is able to make a contribution to his or her community'.

Notice that nowhere in this definition is it describing mental illness – there's a whole other definition for that. When I talk about mental health I'm talking about what makes us thrive and excel, what makes us successful (whatever that means to you) and what allows us to feel fulfilled and productive.

There are quite a few versions of a mental health continuum out there (Delphis, 2020), but I like the simple scale from Crisis on one end, leading to Struggling, Survival in the middle, and on the other end, Thriving and Excelling as visions of good mental health (Figure 2.1).

In most workplaces – even the best-intentioned ones – the mental health agenda is focused on people who are actively struggling. Mental health training is about noticing signs and symptoms of poor mental health, risk-assessing

FIGURE 2.1   The mental health continuum

someone who is emotional, suicidal or withdrawn and providing a range of benefits for the individual to access (often through a convoluted intranet with a well-being page saying something like 'It's OK not to be OK'). I saw a great opening line on a well-intentioned global business's intranet, saying 'Do you struggle with low mood? Are you anxious? We're here to help.'

While there is nothing inherently wrong with pitching help in this way, making mental health part of the disability department, and asking people relentlessly if they're OK (in that downward lilt that is expecting a slow-rolling tear or admittance of pain to make you feel *successful* in your role as a mental health ally) often perpetuates stigma without meaning to. It's saying that mental health is only relevant to people who are struggling, are falling apart or may not be able to do their jobs well. They are labelled as risks, problems, people who should be monitored. By simply having awareness of these crises, organizations convince themselves that they are successful at handling the mental health agenda.

The trouble is, when someone is finally brave enough to seek help – perhaps prompted by someone in HR or a helpful manager pointing them in the direction of a helpline – make no mistake, by the time the cracks are beginning to show at work this individual is likely to be highly distressed or chronically burnt out and there's a reason it's taken them this long to seek support. Perhaps they're in denial about what's going on for them, just trying to keep their head above water at work or feel the stigma of saying they're not OK so have tried keeping the mask up as long as humanly possible.

They then call a helpline, which they are told is confidential. People rarely believe this even though it is broadly true. They're then asked for varying details in order to triage them to the right support, which will be in touch soon. This of course makes sense as a way of seeing which company needs to pay for the support but, from the client's experience, this often adds to their worries about the support being confidential. The experience to someone who has finally been brave enough to seek help is often that of being read a script, rather than showing empathy or care.

Once an individual does get through these barriers, of course there are plenty of examples of useful help they can then receive. It's just interesting that the back end of this industry is insurance based. If a company is on a pay-as-you-go model, the assessing counsellor, who is employed by the EAP, will offer the maximum number of sessions; if the company is on a fixed-rate contract, the client will often be offered the least number of sessions to make the business viable. Unless it's an emergency, the client's need is rarely the focus of this decision.

Having free counselling as a benefit from your company is a wonderful thing in a world of long waiting lists and expensive healthcare. However, the structure, language and process often act as barriers, which is why (on average) usage of this benefit in a post-pandemic world rose only from 10.4 per cent to 11.4 per cent for some companies in the UK (REBA, 2022). Personally, I think this is quite a high percentage compared with what I've seen in some companies I've worked in, where the average is often 6 per cent.

There are a few reasons for this. First, people don't know what the acronym EAP even stands for, so why would they know when to use it?

Second, the information is often talked about once and then hidden within a confusing intranet and third, people tell themselves they're just not 'bad enough yet' to warrant support and so they wait and wait and unfortunately, some people will never get the support they need. Oh, and fourth, people don't trust it. They think information is going back to their company and due to stigma, they worry this could impact their future success.

What we need here is to radically rebrand how we pitch our benefits and the education we offer our people about utilizing this support well before crisis, as a way of maintaining good mental health – this will radically reduce long-term absence due to poor mental health and burnout, reducing people's desire to resign and leave their jobs in the process.

Reliance on technology and a word on culture

Helplines are not the only benefit on offer these days. There are apps springing up all over the place that will help you help yourself while offering data to companies on the biggest challenge areas when it comes to the well-being of their people – ideally in the hope that this data will inform initiatives and support they continue to offer for you, the employee.

I'm all for using apps and technology to support our mental health, to track physical health and to give us access to support through easy video or chat counselling. I can even get on board with artificial intelligence (AI) as a useful initial tool to help people understand themselves better. However, in the workplace this is often seen as THE solution and the onus is fully on the individual to use these tools to optimize their effectiveness. This goes without any consideration for the overall culture: whether there is psychological safety, what the leadership style is, the vision, working practices, purpose, and crucially, a focus on human connection and belonging in a hybrid world.

What is psychological safety? Harvard's Amy Edmondson coined the term in a 1999 journal article focusing on the relationship to team learning and performance. She defines it as a 'shared belief held by the team that the team is safe for interpersonal risk taking.' From a mental health perspective this would translate as a safe space to be open about what's really going on for you without fear of judgement or reprisal. This generally happens with a witness, a colleague, manager or HR professional who can give you space to say what you need to say. We don't build trust through apps. We can utilize apps for self-help and in some cases enhance connection; however, trust is built through the small actions by people that stack every day.

What I'm seeing in companies I work with is that engagement with these benefits is at an all-time low and tech companies that have had huge investments are scrambling to ensure people engage with their tool or method so they can scale as promised to their investors. The reality is, in a hybrid world, that meeting culture and working across time zones means people are feeling the void that technology has left them – a hangover from months of isolation and habits that make tech central to every aspect of our lives – and are longing for space to flourish and feel human again.

While I'm the first to note that technology has helped us stay connected through lockdowns and allows me to stay in touch with family who live overseas, I'm also noting that the rise of depression is really a crisis of connection and the question I'm left with is how do we effectively connect and find a feeling of belonging in our workplaces to support good mental health? What many of these approaches are doing is focusing on the crisis end of the mental health continuum rather than also thinking about creating work environments where people can feel like they're excelling and thriving – and we need more than technology to help us do that.

As Deepak Chopra and Rudolph E Tanzi highlight in their book *Super Brain* (2013) 'Your brain is remodeling itself right now. It doesn't take an injury to trigger the process – being alive is enough.' He goes on to remind us that while we used to think about our brain function being broadly hardwired after infancy, we now know that development is possible throughout our entire lives, going on to say 'Neuroplasticity is better than mind over matter. It's mind turning into matter as your thoughts create new neural growth.'

Now I'm no neuroscientist but doesn't that effectively mean that anything is possible? Nothing is fixed. However, what we tend to do in our cultures is stick in our habit comfort zone. We are the hamster on the wheel never going anywhere, just spinning around and around. If neuroplasticity is to be believed isn't that the absolute worst thing we can do to our mental health as well as our career path? To stay stuck in one neural process so that our brain atrophies and no longer expands to the depths of its still untapped potential.

Of course technology can help but, broader than that, it's practising bravery and putting ourselves in new experiences that develops our brain. So why aren't we leaning in and asking each other different questions? Why aren't we getting more creative than 'How are you?', 'I'm fine'. Why aren't we taking the first brave step to connect with people and be open about our stories rather than outsourcing to helplines and apps?

This, my friends, is what a mentally healthy culture is made of.

Brave people who are expanding their potential every day.

Therapies that need modernizing

Even therapy isn't changing as fast as the world is and while there are some great innovations in therapies – somatic body therapy being one of them – and more knowledge on the impact of trauma on our well-being, so many of us are still trusting our mental health to a psycho-analytical system coined by Freud as early as 1896, going in circles talking about the bad things that happened to us over and over, rather than nurturing the wonder of our brain's neuroplasticity highlighted by developments in neuroscience.

Someone came to me recently for some advice and said 'I've been in therapy for three years; it started by focusing on losing my mother and dealing with the grief of that. It became about loads of childhood trauma and I've been talking about it for two years now. It doesn't feel great – do I need to keep retelling the story of my trauma in order to be OK? How do I tell the therapist that I want a break when there's obviously so much work to do?'

Obviously the decision was up to them, but I offered some observations. I noticed a fear narrative: that if they didn't do the therapy work right now then they'd have hell to pay later – they implied they weren't brave or doing it right if they didn't do it now – which seemed to me like someone else's thinking (anything binary like right/wrong, good/bad is often a thread from society/parents/religion). I asked what their gut was telling them and they took a moment and said: 'I want to take a break and then try out some other kinds of therapies over time'. They had the wisdom within them but this fixation with what was the right thing to do or what would prevent more pain later (a trajectory no one could accurately predict) was keeping them frozen in the pain of telling their story on repeat, with no real route to learning how to thrive in the here and now, even though they have a story.

As I said before, we all have a story and while I really think it's useful to go back into it to understand our patterns of behaviour and own who we are, when we are giving away our agency to others – even professionals – we're losing a crucial piece of the puzzle – our own thoughts on the matter.

And then there's how each of us take responsibility for this conversation in our lives as a whole and at work. When was the last time you asked a friend what's one thing that they're grateful for? When was the last time you asked someone what's going well or what's helping them thrive? When was the last time you asked for a walk and talk meeting, and said out loud what benefits you derived for your mental health by changing up your working day?

We're so focused on the media's skewed view of what the world is like that we forget that we're allowed to be OK, that we're allowed to hold each other accountable for maintaining good mental health and helping each other thrive. It's like we've all collectively accepted the narrative that life is a struggle and perpetuate this narrative every day through the conversations *we* begin.

In my team at PVL anyone at any level of the business will ask each other these types of questions. If we get stuck in a negative loop someone is bound to disrupt the cycle by saying 'I wonder if we should all step back for a minute and think of one thing we're grateful for.' We'll ask each other how we're investing in our mental health that day and we know that that doesn't mean 'are you depressed?'. It means 'did you sleep well, what are your relationships like, have you worked out, did you take time for nutrition, meditation, therapy (or whatever else is supporting that person at the moment)?'

Positive psychology is the scientific study of what makes life most worth living and from where I'm sitting we need a lot more of this injected into our lives in general – but specifically our work lives.

What if work was good for your mental health, not just something you had to recover from later?

Discuss as a team what that might look like and what's in your control to help you change things. Anyone can be the change and ask these sorts of questions. You can have a voice and influence your world around you or – as I see so many times – you can complain, suffer and become a victim of your circumstance as I once was, blaming the world, the economy, your industry, your boss and everything around you for how you feel. Or you can have some agency in your life and make some decisions to do better things – no matter how tiny they are.

As Victor Frankl so eloquently puts it in his book *Man's Search for Meaning* (1946/2004), written after his time in Auschwitz where he was to lose his father, mother and wife to disease or extermination, 'everything can be taken from a man but one thing: the last of the human freedoms – to choose one's attitude in any given set of circumstances, to choose one's own way.'

Leadership and their responsibility for well-being at work

This is even more vital if you're a leader! I will often ask for a show of hands when I speak to groups of senior leaders and executives. I'll say 'Raise your hand if you invest in yourself in some way'. Ninety-five per cent of the room will put their hands up. I'll then say 'Keep your hand up if your team knows when and what you do because it's in your calendar and you talk about it'. Maybe 5 per cent of the room will keep their hand up.

The simplest thing we can do is lead by example and that doesn't just mean openness about when we're struggling (although that's part of it too!). It also means being brave enough to say when things are going right or what we're doing about the struggle. The calendar that I share with my team shows my meetings with my therapist, my gym time and the time I take off to be with my kids. I tell my team when my PTSD is acting up, and crucially, what I need or am doing about it.

As outlined earlier, at PVL we ask each other clear and direct questions that divert from the classic 'How are you?' or 'How was your weekend?'. We ask what's going well and what we are grateful for. Why gratitude? There is extensive research on why focusing on even the smallest things that we're grateful for can impact our overall well-being for good, including increasing resilience, strengthening social relationships and reducing depression. Grateful people report more life satisfaction and it's simply a case of neuroplasticity – the more you focus on something the more it stays in your brain and has a chance to inform your habits. Essentially gratitude changes your brain for good (Young, nd).

A leader also has more impact on working practices than any policy ever will. I am constantly asking for audio calls instead of Zoom meetings so that I can walk and talk, so that I can create a lifestyle that is good for my health. The simple act of doing this gives the rest of the team permission to request similar changes and creates a positive ripple effect in our work culture.

When I set out to start PVL it was born out of total frustration. I worked in youth mental health and corporate well-being for years and, after a little bit of excitement and the promise of innovation, my ideas would be capped and I would notice that we talked a good game as a company but didn't put our words into action. In fact, I've worked in ridiculously toxic places that were advising other organizations on the well-being of their people!

I'd led a double life my whole life and I simply couldn't do it any more. So I set out to figure out the question – could we build a business that did what it told other people to do? That used our team as a test case for building a truly mentally healthy culture. And while it's not a simple ride (it takes slowing down, bravery and action) I believe it is possible. We don't need a mental health network, for example, because everyone is responsible for mental health.

The most junior members of the team frequently ask senior leaders how our mental health is and challenge us to invest in ourselves! I love it. The specific dynamics may be different for your organization, but this level of transparency and communication always makes a difference.

Finally, a mentally healthy culture has two components that need to work together in order to create an environment that can be good for our health and ultimately sustain our individual and organizational success. It takes organizational responsibility as well as individual responsibility.

Organizational responsibility includes creating a culture that makes it safe to talk about the tough stuff, including mistakes made or challenges addressed. It means providing resources and benefits if possible, and crucially, giving leaders the skills to lead by example and have conversations about well-being as a matter of course – not just when there's a crisis and not just during performance reviews or formal meetings. Training and space for thinking about how we work is crucial for getting the environment right.

Second, we need individual responsibility – each and every one of us being brave enough to talk about what's good, the health of our mind, the things that make us struggle (which could be outside of work) and to invest in the maintenance of our mental health. If our work is having a positive impact on our health then this could be part of the maintenance plan: thriving in our skill set, a great routine, a strong community, space to connect and feel a shared sense of direction and purpose, can all be great for our well-being and mental health.

We might need to call that helpline or access support services and we do that because we know ourselves, we take time to reflect and nurture our own ability to critically assess what we need by listening to our body, understanding our story and putting in the work to invest in ourselves. This doesn't have to be heavy or difficult! It often seems like the well-being industry is capitalizing on our unease: it tells us a million and one things we need to do when really the most crucial thing we can do is listen to ourselves and experiment with what feels right for us! We can have fun with it – for example, we can still socialize while also being aware of the amount we drink, and we can have adventures and truly switch off while loving what we do when back at work. We can have boundaries with others but replace what we say no to with things that make us feel great.

A thought on mental illness. You may be reading this thinking 'well, I don't fall into this category'. You might have a chemical imbalance, a diagnosis, a physical health issue or a host of other barriers that would prevent you from taking responsibility for yourself – I've dedicated Chapter 4 fully to this topic so if this applies to you please feel free to jump over to that chapter. Personally I believe we can take responsibility for ourselves no matter what situation we're in! What this looks like can be vastly different for each individual but the principle applies – educate yourself, learn to think for yourself, get advice of course, take medication if necessary, but do it because it feels right for you, not because anyone else told you – more on that later!

In summary, even the best intentions when it comes to the mental health agenda – the ones who've been through something, the ones who want to help, the well-being professionals – are often inadvertently marginalizing the conversation to one of illness and crisis. We've become reactive and are focusing our attention on the struggle, whereas in the words of Martin Seligman (2006), the founder of Positive Psychology, 'The aim of positive psychology is to catalyze a change in psychology from a preoccupation only with repairing the worst things in life to also building the best qualities in life.'

What if success is focusing on where we want to go – not just when it comes to status, wealth or achievement – but on how we want to feel, how healthy we want to be and who we want to have around us. Is that in your 10-year plan?

In order to do this effectively, we need to learn to think for ourselves. You may think you always think for yourself, but what is an original thought and how much are we influenced by conditioning from our past, media narratives and social norms that influence how we show up in the world? How do you know which advice to take when even professionals can have differing views on what you need? My unique perspective on being raised in a cult and then seeing groupthink play out in the workplace informs the next chapter and will enable you to apply all the well-being information out there in a way that is most useful for you!

CHAPTER THREE

Learning to think for ourselves

Is there such a thing as an original thought?

How do we know what we're truly thinking and what's influenced by others?

How do we know that our thoughts are our own and they're not just shaped by our past – our conditioning, our family, the media, generational trauma and other influences?

Well, mostly we are just a walking, talking repeat of our past. This applies to influences but also to genetics, environment, culture, sibling dynamics and a host of other things that influence who we are. This is why I actually do love psychology, it helps us make sense of all those influences. The old school of thought held that somewhere between toddlerhood and the age of 25 our brain would hardwire and it was no longer easy to learn new things. Sayings such as 'I'm just stuck in my ways' are just messages that we repeat to ourselves and then hardwire simply because we believe them so doggedly. Neuroscientist Dr Joe Dispenza (2012) outlines this process in great depth stating that 'the latest research supports the notion that we have a natural ability to change the brain and body by thought alone' going as far as outlining how we can change our genetic code and effectively heal ourselves.

So this means we can learn to think for ourselves and we have more control over how we experience life than we thought. Check out his book in the reference section to go deep on the research.

Have you ever thought that you keep *attracting* the same kind of people into your life? That you *keep* being bullied in the workplace even though you've changed jobs five times? That the same financial troubles keep showing up at your door because you're just unlucky? That your bosses are *always* infuriating micromanagers even though you keep changing departments? Their exact nature may vary, but we all perpetuate patterns in our life based on our own conditioning, perspective and past experiences.

At some point we have to ask ourselves – and psycho-therapy can be a great help here – 'what part am I playing in setting my life up this way?' I am not saying that we all start from the same baseline and have the ability to change anything we want. Narratives that suggest that you can be anything you want are dangerous as they fail to take into account privilege and discrimination (whether this is caused by race, gender, sexuality, class or other factors). There is no simple formula that works for everyone in the same way.

However, the question still holds true. What part am I playing in the repeat patterns I find myself in? When someone tells me they consistently get bullied at work regardless of where they are, it's usually the case that they experienced bullying in their past and this dynamic is a repeat pattern in their friendships and overall life. You could say this behaviour is familiar to them even though it's unhealthy and that we are drawn to what's familiar – a deep-seated better-the-devil-you-know vibe. As an addict myself the first step is always to admit that there's a problem and to practise some radical honesty, and sometimes get some psychological help to understand the pattern that is playing out for you.

Of course this is nuanced and I'm in no way victim-blaming. What I am saying is that in our lives we consistently repeat patterns of behaviour without even thinking about why we're doing it. In a work meeting (well before I started PVL) I observed a difference of opinion play out to the point of escalating into an uncomfortable conflict. Neither side was definitively right or wrong but neither side could fathom why the other person had the opposite view. So convinced by their world view and belief system (influenced of course by family, education and group norms, and these days, algorithms) that they were frustrated the other person simply couldn't see what they could see.

But they saw what they saw because of their conditioning and patterns of behaviour. Their brainwashing if you will and the groupthink that influenced their environments.

I'm sure if you take a minute to reflect back on your life, you may just be able to see patterns such as arguments you generally have, ideas you tend to defend and interactions you repeat, even though the people you have them with are different – and if you go deeper with a therapist and go through your story, you will probably find patterns connected to how your parents behaved, hurt or fear you experienced as a child repeating as a script in your adult life. If you're looking to improve the independence of your thoughts and choices, you need to first have a clear understanding of your patterns and where they come from.

What are brainwashing and groupthink?

In order to understand how to think for ourselves we need to take a brief look at what makes us stop thinking for ourselves. While these terms may seem extreme and were actually coined as a response to the experience of prisoners of war (POWs), my experience of growing up in a cult, working long and hard to find my own true thoughts and subsequently realizing how few people were truly free in the modern world, makes me think these terms are more relevant today than ever before.

The term 'brainwashing' was originally coined during the Korean war in the 1950s and is defined in the Oxford Dictionary (nd) as '[the process of pressurizing] someone into adopting radically different beliefs by using systemic and often forcible means'. This conjures up all sorts of images of violence and torture but in my experience pressurizing doesn't need to be physical. Instead it's the systemic punishment and reward that can be as simple as threatening to push you out of the group and rewarding you with love when your belief system is in line with everyone else's.

I was certainly indoctrinated consistently throughout my childhood, reading only approved propaganda – first in the form of comic books and pictures, later in long letters that were seen as the word of God, and afterwards through public shame, punishment and toxic behaviours.

The threat of brainwashing is actually closer to our society than you think. Our kids as young as two have free rein to access an online world that instructs them to consume, tells them they're not enough and rewards their dopamine centres. It tells them what success looks like (rich), what to aspire to (thin) and who to be (ideally a YouTuber or celebrity perpetuated by our obsession with reality shows and modern-day Cinderella stories). They're isolated, spending more time alone in their rooms, with less real-life experience that boosts resilience and more fear about the world they live in than ever before. This is the brainwashing that starts long before they enter the workforce.

In 1952, William H Whyte created the term 'group-think', which he defined as 'a rationalized conformity – an open, articulate philosophy which holds that group values are not only expedient but right and good as well' (Whyte, 1952). He observed groups of executives using precisely the same methods and the exact same direction in their endeavours, from the cars they would buy, the suits they would own, the type of drink they had on hand and where they lived.

Basically, in order to be seen as an executive in the corporate world at that time, they had to behave like one, and that included how they looked (and many other elements of their lifestyle).

I wouldn't have used any of these terms myself growing up. I didn't think I was in a cult, much less an environment where groupthink was perpetuated, but that's the thing – if it's rationalized conformity then you don't know it's happening when you're in it – it's totally rational to you! Truly effective groupthink leaves its participants convinced that they are thinking for themselves.

We all like to think that we're a picture of free will and have nobly chosen the path we're on but many of us follow the same course. We get into ridiculous amounts of student debt in order to secure that status-fuelled job, aim to find the perfect partner for life, maybe have a couple of kids we now need lots of money to raise, and don't forget that mortgage, which will tie you right down for the next 40 years, and we wonder why people stay in toxic jobs. They genuinely feel like they don't have a choice. They have rationalized their conformity in such a way that the only way their body can scream 'help' is by getting them sick, burnt out, anxious or depressed.

I'm not suggesting that this path is wrong, in fact, some people will find happiness this way, but have you ever thought about why we all think this is the one way to live in western society? Aren't we just following on blindly from history? Why aren't we questioning things or asking ourselves how we truly want to live this one short, precious life?

Other societies have a different set of rules, norms that they also follow simply because that's just the way it is. It's like we've all set up a secret pact to keep safe, to play a part in capitalism and to ultimately keep the peace and belong – but is it really belonging when nobody gets to see who you truly are?

In order for groupthink to work it's important to have a narrative that is prepared to counter any objections that may arise. I grew up on the extreme end of this – whole narratives were repeated on a daily basis that would counter any allegation that anything untoward was happening. Whenever something good happened, credit was given to the leaders or belief system of the cult while, whenever something bad happened, then you took the blame and could see any pain as a rightful punishment from God. This experience indoctrinates its victims through fear – particularly the fear of being alone.

I see this all the time in organizations. They celebrate collective wins as a *we* – we have such a great product, leadership or organization – and then blame the individual if they are burnt out, depressed or not able to bring their full self to the work table. Losing your job brings with it plenty of shame, from the secret way human resources will manage someone out, or when someone has to leave on the spot (garden leave), once a trusted member of the team and now looked at with total suspicion, all passwords changed and no longer part of the tribe. Work can form your identity, purpose, work ethic and belief system, it can be your social hub, your friendship network and your financial security – we stop questioning groupthink as we don't want to be the odd one out. The threat of being kicked out of the tribe taps into a primal fear, one that historically would have meant destitution and death.

The world of work is changing. People are voting with their feet. Terms such as 'the great resignation' highlight the post-Covid economic trend, in which employees are voluntarily resigning en masse for reasons such as wage stagnation, dissatisfaction with their work and wanting a greater work–life balance. A recent survey by LifeWorks (Allen, 2020) outlines that 76 per cent of workers say the way an organization supports their mental health is a key factor in whether or not they will stay, with the younger generation stating many additional pressures impacting their mental health. One foundational aspect of supporting good mental health is getting good sleep, with social media use connected to decreased and disrupted sleep, which is associated with depression, memory loss and poor performance (McLean Hospital, 2022). Other challenges include a competitive job market, fear of missing out, assuming everyone else's life is perfect and a lot more time being isolated or alone.

Make no mistake though, we also have more opportunity than we've ever had. The internet affords anyone, young or old, to work independently, grow a business or side hustle and learn anything they want to learn! And while this can be used for immense good, giving the possibility of financial freedom to all sorts of marginalized people, it can also suck you into a vortex of feeling not good enough and overwhelmed with advice on how to live your life.

So much noise to wade through in order to have a true original thought.

When you're faced with a crossroads or big decision what do you generally do? For many of us, we might start discussing our options with a trusted friend, we may ask parents for advice, we might listen to a podcast, read a book or perhaps even discuss with a therapist or coach. These days many people will scroll their social feeds for hackable advice, inspiration, motivation or advice from an influencer who has no idea what your situation is. If we really look within, we probably already know what we want to do but that may be scary or against the grain so we often convince ourselves that making the decision according to social norms is the best option in the end. We remind ourselves about where we should be at different stages of our life and measure ourselves against these extremely narrow expectations. No wonder so many people are experiencing what is termed a quarter-life crisis in their 30s – that period of questioning where they feel trapped and disillusioned, wondering what the point of anything is.

When was the last time you heard someone say 'I'm at a crossroads, I have a decision to make – I'm going to switch off my social media for 48 hours and take some time to really reflect on what my body feels is the right decision'? No wonder we are spiralling and never quite hit the mark of our expectations – no wonder we're lonelier and more depressed than ever before: according to the World Health Organization (2021), depression was already the leading cause of disability worldwide prior to the Covid-19 pandemic and has skyrocketed since.

In Daniel Pick's book *Brainwashed* (2022), he discusses the terms 'brainwashing' and 'groupthink' with a group of adolescents – when contemplating technology and social media they commented that:

> Online resources have been engineered... not only to be convenient and replete with creative tools but also to be extremely addictive... The set-up is constantly honed to be more and more engrossing and hard to leave, even if nobody compels [or brainwashes] us. It is designed to capture our desire for contact with friends, to see what happens when we dare to throw a thought out there into the world and discover who responds, and in what numbers...

Pick goes on to comment in the part titled 'Groupthink' that 'no one is immune to the varieties of influence and persuasion communicated relentlessly over months and years', categorizing the account of this process throughout history. From war propaganda and defining a woman's place in society to activism and movements for change – we are influenced by the collective narrative on what is important and what to be part of.

Not all workplaces are toxic, however, all workplaces and society at large need an element of groupthink to function. Shared narratives, purpose, values and slogans are all ways to keep people motivated to perform in the right direction – while keeping them stuck in a narrative that the higher up you get the more you can consume and there's no way you could go back to living a different life now. It's forward action or nothing. You have people relying on you now – a partner perhaps, kids, that dream house to pay for. In my days as a therapist, I heard all the reasons repeated ad nauseum while my client was simultaneously falling apart.

To balance out this narrative, we do need a little bit of groupthink in order to survive, to work cohesively and create tribes to help us thrive – McDougall (1985) high-lights that 'the infant's narcissism has to be punctured' – in other words, as a baby we get to be totally self-absorbed, in fact we need to be to survive, however, in later life we need to learn how to become interdependent, to listen and work alongside others in order to be successful in life. So we all need a little groupthink in order to survive, however, the extreme of being too agreeable or a 'chameleon can give rise to clinical concern' according to McDougall. This is something many of us end up doing – including me! I became a chameleon, wearing a mask in order to survive, adapting to whatever anyone else thought was normal and making them believe I was like them. Balance is key. We need collective ideas to enhance our well-being but if we give up our right to think completely, our well-being and path to success (whatever that really means to you) can be thwarted.

And so we turn to the narratives on mental health and well-being – the height of which is both a reaction to the times we're in and a persuasion to stay distracted from the key challenges. We are experiencing information overload even here – impacting people's ability to think for them-selves and create the environments that will enable them to thrive.

There's masses of information out there and countless experts who have the one formula for what you should do to get well, optimize health, manage depression, solve trauma, cure anxiety, and on and on the list goes. The untrained or vulnerable eye can be bounced from pillar to post on things to do and think about so even finding the right solution can take on a feeling of overwhelm and neurosis.

I had a question after a talk I did recently at a FinTech company where a young woman stood up and said:

> I'm trying to do all the things and I just can't keep it up.
> When I'm not doing something I feel guilty and it seems
> like everyone else is waking up at 5 am like Robin Sharma
> advises, taking cold showers Wim Hof style, meditating,
> journalling, exercising, doing yoga, having a bedtime routine,
> spending the right time with the right friends, having a job
> that fulfils them and I just feel like I'm getting it wrong – like
> I'm being left behind. My anxiety is worse than it's ever been.

Poor girl, I thought! No wonder she's anxious!

I commented that even the well-being space is trapped in hustle culture and information overload. We are left with this gnawing feeling – 'when I do all the things just right THEN I'll get to this destination, I'll be cured, I'll have solved the struggle, I'll be confident, and maybe I'll even ask for that promotion or change my job.' Too many of us feel that we are not *enough* as we currently are.

And while I was raised in the classic 'sacrifice now, do the work now for heavenly rewards later' mindset, our brains respond well to being part of a tribe and working forever towards a distant goal of success – which of course changes every time we achieve our destination. While modern society offers us so many resources and opportunities, we are still the most depressed we have been because of the perpetuation of this 'I'm currently not doing enough' mindset, which is amplified by social media, comparisons and hustle culture.

And while I agree with Shawn Achor (2011), the eminent positive psychologist, who said 'Happiness is a work ethic.

It's something that requires our brains to train just like an athlete has to train', I sometimes wonder if we're trying to do everyone else's training instead of our own and if we're missing a crucial point, that the work ethic needs to be ours and ours alone. It must be influenced by our body, our mind and our needs – not the needs of everyone else on the planet.

I know you want solutions. If you've picked up this book, then there's a good chance that you want to fix something in your life. Maybe you're looking for a professional to give you some insight, a plan, a framework, a thing to do. Well, the greatest insight I can give you is a path to enhance your self-awareness. No one can be aware for you, you're the one in your life, living out your patterns and perpetuating your belief systems. While we have a well-being industry that has names, labels, supplements, medication and frameworks for practically everything, don't forget that only you live in your body, live in your head and can sense, deep down if something feels right for you.

While this sounds simple it isn't easy. Especially if you, like me, have to unpick a lifetime of brainwashing, coercion and groupthink in order to belong or fit in. I realize these phrases sound extreme if you lived a regular life of going to school and being set on the path, but that path has definitions of those words too. It's no longer the extreme PoW camps where these ideas take place but the slow drip effect of advertising, media spin and social media algorithms that repeat your small world back to you.

When I left the cult I thought I would be free by default – but I wasn't. I took my thoughts with me. It can take years to overcome the impact that a toxic situation can have on your mind and even longer to truly come back to thinking for yourself. If you've experienced a toxic workplace, an abusive manager or any difficult job in the past, it's highly likely that this experience is still having an impact on your mental well-being, confidence or outlook on life.

Fear has a lot to answer for when it comes to how we live our lives.

With the best intentions of keeping us safe, the survival experience has been greatly exaggerated in a post Covid-19 world. The long-term impact for many of us is that our fight or flight safety response has been hijacked by 24-hour news notifications and the impending threat of death, making us cling harder to a tribe or place where we can belong – and thereby stay safe – even if it means giving up our thinking.

From how intensely we quarantined and bought into everything we were told, to political sides, vax debates, protests and causes – one thread ran through people's experience – pick a side! Pick your truth and stick with it – even though we were aware of the amount of misinformation and conflicting reports, still people vehemently fought their sides at dinner parties, on social media, and lost friends over differing opinions.

To me, the most important thing I can teach my children is critical thinking. To be aware of misinformation, to read everything with a question mark in their mind and to question anyone propagating the idea of one truth or one way. Having a fixed idea of something being totally true simply doesn't take into account the complexity of being human, the nuanced rainbow of colours that impacts any type of truth – perspective, the lens someone looks through, their historical and generational trauma lens, the information they've had available to them, the list goes on and on.

So when I see a guru, coach or well-being professional telling me they have the one thing or the three steps or the simple formula, immediately I hold in my mind the privilege of doubt. I don't run away in fear, throwing out everything they say – I weigh up what they're saying against what feels right for me. It's taken a long time for me to be able to respect their process of truth, listen with an open heart and then take in the one small thing that may be true for me.

This is what I mean by critical thinking. It's not throwing out everything and becoming paranoid – it's being able to practise the art of holding everything lightly, weighing it up, listening to your body and your needs and adopting what feels right for you in that moment. No truth lasts a lifetime. Our bodies change, our minds evolve and the circumstances around us mean we need different things – and with this in mind, our well-being practices can evolve over time and so too can our definition of success.

I used to meditate for three minutes every day when I had just quit drinking because it helped me emotionally regulate; I then left meditation alone for years and later revisited it in a completely different way. What worked for you before, during and after the pandemic are probably different – that's OK. Experiment with what works for you.

The meditation coach Emily Fletcher in her interview on the Aubrey Marcus Podcast (2022) said 'using an app to meditate is like going to an AA meeting in the middle of a liquor store... it's like walking into the belly of the beast when really you want to connect with yourself.' This made me laugh, not least because I'm an alcoholic, but also because it reiterated for me that all of our attempts to unplug are often structured using the very devices and platforms that we are trying to unplug from – it's hilarious if you think about it.

Even though this rings true for me (that apps aren't the best path to meditation), that doesn't make it THE truth. It doesn't make us wrong or bad if we decide to use an app or go down a different path. This shows how coerced thinking can have an influence in any space, even well-being. Just when you think you've got a balance for you, some new information comes in to knock you off your truth and make you think you're doing it wrong – even when we're working on ourselves, we are still tempted by the need to conform and adapt to other people's approaches. We're hustling at our feelings and our thoughts when really, they just are, they're just a script, often based on fear and conditioning, and it does take Shawn Achor's idea of training the mind to stay alert and mentally healthy – but also, training can be fun.

It's not all military precision and effort, it's holding humour at how hilarious and mixed up we are as humans, how little we actually know, and observing our need to hold on tightly to a belief system or ideology of life – it's as if we think that if we hold on to an idea strongly enough and defend it with our energy, then there won't be as much uncertainty in the world! But what if it's the act of holding on tightly, giving away our agency and being open to relentless amounts of information, which we eventually have to numb out in order to survive, which is actually making us sick!

What if the rise in depression, anxiety and all manner of physical and mental health difficulties is really a life lived on someone else's blueprint until we don't even know what our blueprint is any more. When someone used to ask me what I needed I had no idea how to answer that! When I first studied coaching and was asked in a practice session 'What do you want – what do you really want?' this was such a foreign concept to me that I had no idea what to say!

Nurturing curiosity and learning from others is key to our learning, growth and evolution as humans. This may seem counter to my argument about groupthink, information overload and social media influencing our well-being – but it's actually a crucial skill to enable us to think for ourselves. The New Economics Foundation highlighted learning as one of the five key ways to well-being (Aked et al, 2008), and more than ever it's imperative that we open our minds to new ways of thinking and being. Our world views are closing in more than ever as advertisers hit us with exactly what they think we want and target messages and stories at us that will reinforce our world view and ensure that we continue to buy – so it takes conscious effort and will to listen to alternative opinions, read things from a different perspective and spend time with people who are different from us.

Curiosity can be playful. It can be doing something outside of your comfort zone, speaking to someone new, really listening to their story, disrupting the 'how-are-you-I'm-fine' ping-pong effect, and above all, this curiosity will help you develop neuroplasticity, essentially changing your brain and giving you more resources to be mentally healthy. Curiosity helps us influence our world for the better rather than staying stuck in a narrative of why things are hard. It gives us possibilities and can give us options with which to reflect, so we can decide what is true for us.

So, you may say, this is all well and good if you have the energy and resource to think and make these decisions and take the required action – but what if you don't? What if your mental health has taken a hit, you're burnt out and all the notions of work–life balance simply don't do the trick any more. What if you can barely get through the day, much less get curious and find time to reflect. Well, in the next chapter I'll help you assess where you're at, explore the first steps, which can include getting help, and set you on the curious path to thinking for yourself.

If you have a brain it's possible to change it, so stay on the journey with me and let's see where it takes us!

CHAPTER FOUR

Stress, burnout
and mental illness

This is a big subject for a relatively small book.

I'm not going to be able to cover every sign, symptom, or tactic for how to manage or solve these challenges. I want to provide you instead with some useful information and show you how to apply the principles of thinking for yourself even to the area of burnout and mental illness. This is the stage when your actions are no longer preventative but are instead about managing the crisis. I want to connect this topic to the workplace, our environments and our personal responsibility – all of these factors impact our likelihood of success (whatever that means to you).

First of all, the crisis usually shows up because we haven't been listening to what we want or need for months, years or even decades. Stress builds up in our body and while stress can be a great driver and is a natural part of life, the ways in which we shake off this stress to prevent the build-up should be a part of our daily lifestyle, but in modern society, it often isn't. We sit more than we've ever sat, we stare at screens more than we ever have and often transition from our sedentary working day (Teams/Zoom fatigue anyone?) to scrolling on our phones, browsing Netflix or ordering food (and maybe even meditating on an app!).

This means that we often have to make a conscious decision to be active, e.g. going for a walk, a hike or to the gym, with this added effort meaning we move less than we ever have. As a result, our stress stays stuck, not being released but circulating within our bodies waiting to strike when the straw finally breaks the proverbial camel's back.

Stress and burnout

In the book *Burnout* by Amelia Nagoski and Emily Nagoski (2020), they introduce the concept of 'completing your stress cycle' – essentially a way of reducing the stress that gets stuck and instead shaking it off so it doesn't become a problem down the line. They show that burnout isn't cognitive, we can't just think or talk our way through it (this includes traditional talking therapies), instead it's physical or somatic. If we can release the stress then we're good but, if we keep it stored up or 'stuck in the tunnel' as they refer to it, then we're at risk. There are great ways to complete the stress cycle including movement, connection, hugs, laughter, tears, breathing and creativity. When this book came out I read it first and then posted a copy to everyone in our team. We all read it from cover to cover and gained a shared language around burnout, and crucially, its prevention at PVL. We discussed what we learnt from the book in a team meeting and will proactively ask each other 'how are you completing your stress cycle today?' and do our best to fulfil this at work through walk and talk meetings, laughter and connection and positive accountability as a team.

There's a wonderful opportunity in the new world of flexible or asynchronous work for people to invest in themselves at the time of day that works best for them and we practise this at PVL. We're a fully remote team and discuss openly what we're doing to look after ourselves even if it's not during a traditional lunch break. It has to start with me, the CEO, so I can demonstrate through my behaviours that my employees can invest in themselves too. This might include walking a dog, picking up kids, having a therapy session or getting away from our desks for a coffee. People take responsibility to turn their camera off or to walk during a meeting or to challenge someone if they seem to be struggling with their mental health or even their workload. Mental health is everyone's business, not just a well-being lead or HR professional.

The workplace of the future is changing whether we like it or not. People are voting with their feet, taking time off for health reasons or simply changing their lifestyles so that they are healthier. If Covid taught us anything it's that life is short and it's up to us how we live our lives – screw the rules!

In 2019 burnout was defined by the World Health Organization as an occupational phenomenon and added to the International Classification of Diseases list (ICD-11). While it is not classified as a medical condition, this is how the WHO defines burnout:

> ...a syndrome conceptualized as resulting from chronic workplace stress that has not been successfully managed. It is characterized by three dimensions:
>
> • feelings of energy depletion or exhaustion;
> • increased mental distance from one's job, or feelings of negativism or cynicism related to one's job; and
> • reduced professional efficacy.
>
> Burn-out refers specifically to phenomena in the occupational context and should not be applied to describe experiences in other areas of life.

Of course, this doesn't tell the whole story. While this explanation is very much focused solely on work, it doesn't take into account the countless studies citing trauma as playing a key part in the risk factors linked to burnout. Research by Substance Abuse and Mental Health Services Administration (SAMHSA) highlighted that experiencing childhood trauma can increase the risk of burnout later in life. So while burnout may very well be an occupational phenomenon given our always-on culture, the experience is certainly exacerbated by the build-up of unprocessed trauma that remains stuck in our bodies. We should also factor in the trauma of discrimination, racism and war (whether experienced or generational) and add on the collective trauma many of us experienced through the Covid-19 pandemic, and constant news of war and environmental crises. This vicarious trauma alongside our lifestyles is perpetuating the scale of burnout in society today.

There are also a range of symptoms for burnout and it's important that we notice the signs early on and actually change something in our environment or lifestyle. To not do so could see us descend slowly into full-on burnout. There are varying schools of thought when it comes to the recovery time for full-on burnout – these veer from weeks all the way to five years, which speaks to the fact that many of our experiences are different. Dr Geri Puleo (nd) notes that it takes an average of two years to recover from a full burnout episode.

In a world where time is often used as the biggest excuse for not doing something (I don't have time to slow down, change things, invest in myself), people don't realize how much time it takes to drive yourself to burnout and then recover from it. It's just a question of where you want to spend your time – something only you can decide on.

In the 1970s, the American psychologist Herbert Freuden-berger originally coined the word 'burnout'. He went on to develop the 12 stages of burnout, which is a fascinating conversation starter in workshops I've led and it's worth listing them here so you can ask yourself some crucial questions and consider whether any of these stages apply to you.

The 12 stages of burnout are:

1 Compulsion to prove oneself
2 Working harder
3 Neglecting own needs
4 Displacement of conflicts (taking things out on people who have nothing to do with your stress – often loved ones)

5   Revision of values
6   Denial of emerging problems
7   Withdrawal
8   Behavioural changes
9   Depersonalization (feeling like you're outside of yourself, observing yourself)
10 Inner emptiness
11 Depression
12 Burnout syndrome (a combination of many of the above and categorized as extreme physical and emotional exhaustion, cynicism and often a variety of physical symptoms preventing you from focusing and performing as you once did).

Have a look at this list and notice if you've ever moved up or down the list. At what stage do you usually wake up and pull yourself back just a little – for me it's when I get to number four. When I start getting irritable with the people who love me the most, that's my cue to step back, reflect and notice I'm on the road to burnout.

It's amazing how many people will say 'Oh wow, I'm definitely at 6 or 7 now' or 'I've definitely reached number 10 – inner emptiness'. It's also fascinating to note that depression is seen as number 11. It's possible that the skyrocketing rise in depression over the last few years is partly caused by an increase in cases of burnout.

This is why I'm hesitant about the propensity for mental health training at work to be all about noticing signs and symptoms. Many symptoms cross over between things and unless you want to spend years studying the many nuances, it's actually more important to focus on listening and creating a safe place for someone to think for themselves, practise the skill of curiosity and empower them to take the action they believe is right. More on supporting others in Chapter 6.

Let me repeat the key point: everyone is different and this isn't a linear process. However, understanding how burnout can show up can act as a great tool to enhance self-awareness and help you understand your own body and mind.

I've seen that people in caring and support-type professions are particularly at risk of burnout (this can include HR professionals, and mental health or diversity allies at work). One of the key factors that has been researched is what has been coined empathy or compassion fatigue. This is prevalent in a variety of helping professions (such as doctors, nurses, therapists) and has symptoms very similar to those of burnout. 'Empathy fatigue is the emotional and physical exhaustion that comes from caring for people day after day,' says psychologist Dr Susan Albers (Cleveland Clinic, 2021). Coupled with workplace systems that are oppressive in their workload, systems and politics, this phenomenon has been prevalent since the Covid-19 pandemic. But just think about your workplace for a minute and the support roles whose remit has now radically increased – if these are the people the rest of us are going to for support and yet they are experiencing reduced empathy and burnout symptoms themselves, how in the world are we supposed to get the adequate support we need?

Anecdotally, those wonderful passionate internal activists who are constantly supporting others are also experiencing higher levels of burnout. In some businesses I've seen the same two or three people rolled out every awareness day to tell their story of mental illness, racism or brush with suicide, and while it's admirable and wholly useful to tell our stories, if the work culture isn't consistently mentally healthy then this can simply leave these people feeling vulnerable and more at risk of empathy fatigue.

What questions do we each need to ask ourselves about our daily working practices and our support mechanisms in order to create healthier environments? First, take a step back and look at your life from a bird's-eye view. Imagine that you are on Google Maps and then keep on zooming out until you can see your city, your country, the entire globe of your life landscape. Think about your culture, society's expectations, what you think you *should* do, the impact your lifestyle is having on your body and your mind. Zoom in closer and see your immediate environment (this includes living space, workspace, the social energy around you, and your daily habits). Be honest with yourself: how is your world contributing to your burnout levels?

Before you convince yourself that there's nothing you can do about it, remember that it takes two years or more on average to recover from full-on burnout. Do you want to spend the time there or do you want to spend it here and now being honest about where you're at and the contributing factors and then, crucially, asking yourself what is in your control? Some things won't be of course, but there will definitely be a whole range of things that are in your control – how can you begin to take personal responsibility for your situation?

This could include changing your environment, completing your stress cycle as part of your daily routine and sometimes, just sometimes, deciding to leave a toxic environment completely. Sometimes there's a whole lot we can do inside our workplace and we can try those things first to be sure that we've done everything in our power and then, perhaps if we can't change things from within, we need to make the brave decision to leave the situation completely.

Remember, step 5 of the 12 stages of burnout is revision of values – dismissing what used to be important to you in favour of new things. Often we are coerced into believing that the values of our workplace are most important… perhaps leading us to believe that we must work all hours, that we need to say yes to everything to stay afloat and give up our health, happiness and fulfilment to survive. After all, how else will you pay your mortgage, please your spouse, support your family and do 'what's right'?

It's useful to ask yourself what brings you energy and what depletes it both in work and outside of it. Take the bird's-eye view of your life and really look at it honestly and then ask yourself which parts of your situation are your responsibility and can be changed, which parts aren't your responsibility but are influenceable, and which are completely out of your control? For the latter, it may be best to simply let go so that you save the energy for the parts that you can change – even if it goes against society's view of what success looks like.

This doesn't just apply in the corporate world. You may be an entrepreneur trying something new, you may have a hustle and a plan – even when doing purposeful wonderful work, we can get sucked into the cult of busy and think every waking moment needs to be HUSTLING.

My awareness of my body and mind has taught me that sometimes that hustle is a blissful avoidance strategy. I don't want my old trauma to be triggered, I don't want to feel the uncertainty of life and so I just work harder, hustling as if my future is truly in the palm of my hand and couldn't be knocked off its pedestal at any time.

I've also heard from so many clients, friends and colleagues about how their mental health suffers when all of the hustle and control they utilized still couldn't prevent their business failing, relationship imploding or health degrading. This can even happen when we're exiting something great, retiring, or transitioning onto a new career path. Our brain may see what's happening and make sense of it but our nervous system isn't prepared for it, we're wired for busy and to not be busy or numbing our feelings is to be... well, nothing. Our identity shatters, the feelings we've kept at bay come flooding in and we're left drowning in the questions of how to live a good life.

These times can throw us off our balance, descend us into depression, and can also act as the greatest opportunity to question everything – to find out how we actually feel and think about things for ourselves – finally!

Ultimately early burnout symptoms can show up anywhere and to anyone. But whose responsibility is it – is it simply an occupational phenomenon that we can blame on work? Is it caused by our own work–life balance or lack of boundaries and therefore our individual responsibility? When burnout occurs in the workplace it's both – organizations need to think about evolving working practices alongside the changing times and they need to set up structures and give you permission to invest in yourself throughout the working day. And then, each of us has the ultimate responsibility for ourselves and our own mental health and burnout levels! Of course, factors like historical trauma and working in caring professions may make us more at risk, but that just means that we need to be even more aware of our responsibility than others. I say this as a person who has both of those risk factors at play. Either I can hold my hands up and say 'well, I've had XYZ trauma, I'm a CEO, a parent, a therapist, an entrepreneur – there's nothing I can do about it', or I can be fully aware and take responsibility.

I've chosen my work, I've set up my family life, I've learnt about trauma and know how it affects me. I could choose a thousand other paths and yet here I am, in charge of my schedule and my health and responsible for my burnout levels – even if that's meant leaving jobs in the past, saying no to things and occasionally crashing out close to burnout and thinking 'jeez, I did it again – let's take a step back and see what's in my control now and let go of what isn't'.

People think that all well-being professionals are proponents of cutting back, doing less, staring into nature more and reducing our ambitions in order to look after our health. This may seem radical but it's actually not the angle I come from at all. I love ambition, unrealistic goals, work ethic and pushing myself to my limits mentally and physically. I relish the opportunity to do many things in this one life I've been given – but sometimes this drive to help can be the biggest thorn in our side, as we once again lay flat on our backs, broken, burnt out or depressed, thinking this time we'll get this right and sustain success in a way that is healthy!

It's not about doing less. It's about doing the right things for you. Creating your own version of a balanced life that includes active recovery, learning new things, helping your nervous system feel safe and focusing on what gives you energy.

Working on something you love doing doesn't even feel like work, it gives you energy, fulfilment and a sense of purpose – all great attributes for good mental health. Working on something you despise in an environment where you are treated unfairly and have no space to invest in yourself is where the problems begin.

So while there are plenty of ways to prevent burnout, the real skill here is radical honesty! What does my life look like, what gives me energy, what depletes it and what small thing is in my control? Even if it's simply putting the wheels in motion to create change slowly, this will enable you to take back some agency in your life and where you're headed, opening up a whole world of possibility.

Boundaries

A skill to develop to support all aspects of your mental health is one of boundaries. It's your ability to say no, to own your own stuff but leave other people's stuff to them, it's what you need to prioritize your health and manage the amount of noise and bad news that will overwhelm your brain if you're not careful.

I once went on a course that was called 'No is a full sentence'. We had to practise different scenarios where we wanted to say no but would be persuaded by pretend family or friends who had logical reasons for why they needed our help. We simply had to practise saying no without offering extensive reasoning behind our answer.

'Can I borrow money?'
'No' was the only response we could give.
'Can you look after my dog?'
Again, 'no' was all we could practise.

It may seem silly but this was harder than it looked. We felt uncomfortable and wanted to give the person lengthy reasons for why it wouldn't work this time, leaving the door open to be asked again or in a different way.

A boundary can be physical or emotional and applies in our personal life as well as our work life. Emotional or mental boundaries protect your right to have your own feelings and thoughts, to not have your feelings criticized or invalidated, and to not have to take care of other people's feelings (Campbell, 2021).

Having effective boundaries is crucial to a healthy work life in a hybrid world, and yet it takes self-awareness and time to know what boundaries are healthy for you and to experiment with pushing back on other people's demands.

In this new always-on hybrid world the skill of boundaries is more important than ever. It will give us the ability to focus on creative work, stay present with the people who are important to us, maximize efficiency in our job and invest in ourselves even during the working day. Of course, it also needs to be coupled with a communication style that is kind yet clear and holds your individual needs in mind as well as the collective needs of your team or family.

While there is lots of guidance out there on how to set an effective boundary, what people often forget is to communicate this boundary to the people who will be affected by it. They say no to calendar invites for meetings, make time for the gym or therapy, meditate or spend time with their family, etc, but then wonder why there is friction around them – questions or pushback – right through from 'why weren't you at that meeting?' to 'I thought we were going to have dinner at six'.

Putting in boundaries at work or home is a beautiful way to lead by example in creating a healthy lifestyle and preventing burnout or other illnesses, but we're more likely to stick to these endeavours if we also explain to people what we're doing and when we will ensure the deadline is met, family time is focused or a discussion can be had.

At work you can have a conversation about health, meeting culture and what everyone needs to be productive and effective in their jobs. This will not only help people do what's right for them but also prevent the friction that can show up when one person is seen to do these things and the others assume they cannot. This can form the base-line of pushing in the same direction as a team while taking personal and collective responsibility to lead healthier lifestyles.

In a rapidly changing world our boundaries are likely to evolve depending on what is going on around us and that's OK – it just means that taking time to reflect both person-ally and as a team on what's working and what isn't is more crucial than ever.

A key boundary that can be useful for you to set is around the media influences you allow into your life. It is too easy to absent-mindedly allow news notifications or social media to impact our stress response and overall well-being. This is not a 'one size fits all' but for me, I don't have any news notifications and actually rarely watch the news.

I know, I know, you may say you simply must stay abreast of current affairs or your job demands it or you enjoy knowing about all the terrible things happening in the world but it's too easy to become focused on the negatives while not noticing that great things are happening too. In a world that is hyperconnected and measured in clicks, headlines have become more shocking and focused on negativity than ever before, and yet, we still can have a say in what we allow into our brain. Do we want our synapses to get fixed focusing on everything that's terrible or do we want to use the brain's neuroplasticity to focus on what's possible in our world?

Having some boundaries around the news and general media influences gives me greater space to think for myself! I can consciously dip into information that is credible and worthwhile to my learning and development while ignoring the things that will simply make me jumpy, on edge and closer to burnout – yes, social media is designed to get you hooked to perpetuate its success – but you have more choice here than you think.

What's one boundary that will support your overall well-being, and crucially, help you avoid the slippery burnout slope?

Mental illness and success

A question we might ask – can a person with a mental illness still be successful? Is a mental illness a life sentence, is it something that will hold you back, take you off course, make you feel like you're playing catch up while you see others flying – can you still live the life you want, and crucially, does all this talk about thinking for yourself and taking responsibility for your mental health even apply to you?

If you're a leader or a manager and someone tells you that they struggle with a mental health issue, where do your assumptions immediately go? Will they be able to do their work? Am I going to have to find cover for them? Will they be emotional or erratic in the workplace? They're one to watch! Even the more well-intentioned workplaces still perpetuate stigma!

Stigma and fear are the big things that stop us from getting help. We are afraid of judgement, to be outcast, to be misunderstood, to not understand ourselves. No wonder we often wait until we're in crisis to find out what in the world is going on with our mind!

The definition of stigma is 'a mark of disgrace associated with a particular circumstance, quality or person' (Merriam-Webster, nd) and while we have come a long way, stigma still keeps people trapped in their inner world, unable to get help for fear of being ostracized from the group and needing to survive alone. In its most extreme form, stigma can result from shaming someone from a different background, culture or race from us. However, stigma also shows up in subtle ways – it could be making jokes about people with mental health struggles, calling them crazy, nutjobs or worse; in teams we may avoid the person who is struggling with their mental health, gossip about their inability to keep to a deadline or let them go without ever asking them what was going on.

Now don't get me wrong, we need a whole array of professionals at different stages of our life to support our mental health – but when there's this hush-hush way about someone 'seeing someone' or 'getting help' and we are hesitant to ask anything about the experience afterwards, we perpetuate stigma in assuming the whole thing simply shouldn't be spoken about unless absolutely necessary, 'is best left to professionals' and therefore not our problem! I will ask people in my team in my workplace how their therapy is going and they will ask me about mine. Why not? It's up to us which bits we want to share but it's important to normalize the conversation about accessing support and investing in ourselves in order to be successful in life.

At work, if someone takes time off due to a broken leg or a physical health issue like cancer treatment, people at work will speak to them when they return – how are you, how was your hospital stay, it's good to have you back.

In many places, if someone has been off work due to a bout of depression, when they return there will be an awkward atmosphere, they will be ignored, the weather will be discussed, people will avoid eye contact or checking in on how the person actually is.

Even many well-intentioned workplaces will have a mental health champion programme of some kind or a mental health awareness initiative with everything pointing to crisis, helplines and support. Images with people in despair, catchy comms saying 'if you're struggling call this number', disability groups that have a mental health component and everything pointing to the fact that I-don't-want-to-be-part-of-that-quirky-club. Just like people don't want to go to the addiction group at work as they feel they are inadvertently shaming themselves if they do, people don't want to go to the crisis mental health group either.

And so, no wonder we are hesitant to get diagnosed or to investigate what might be going on within our minds and bodies – we're scared of what we'll find and what that will mean for the lives we live!

So what if we're finally in crisis and worried that there's something wrong with our mental health? Here's some insight into people who've gotten to that point and eventually received a diagnosis.

Across my own clients, friends and colleagues who have talked to me about their mental illness there is a vast array of experiences. Some people are so relieved once they have a diagnosis, as finally they know what they are dealing with and can begin to understand themselves better and get the right kind of support. For others, as soon as they are labelled they go into a fixed state, giving away their autonomy to professionals, doctors and family and believing that they simply have a chemical imbalance and must now live with a life sentence – I know people who have attempted to take their lives once they found out what mental illness they had.

There can also simply be confusion about what advice to follow, whether to get second opinions, to stick with a therapist even if it doesn't feel great, to take medication or not and whether it's wise to push yourself at work or stay on the path of your ambitions or success (whatever that means to you).

Remember the mental health continuum I talked you through earlier. Even if you have a diagnosis this fluctuation in how you feel still applies – it doesn't mean you now stay stuck firmly in crisis. Sometimes you may be struggling or in crisis (perhaps to a greater degree than someone without a diagnosis) and sometimes you'll be surviving, thriving and even excelling. Learning to manage your diagnosis, finding space to think for yourself, accessing support and even finding the right balance of medication can all support you to thrive and continue to reach fulfilment and success.

While this transition to understanding may slow you down for a bit, once you've adjusted and evolved what you need to manage well, your ambitions can continue to be pursued – life may even have made you want to evolve them somewhat.

There is no one right way or path when it comes to the health of our minds. The brain is still a vastly unknown frontier with the emergence of new ideas showing up all the time. Just look at Dr Joe Dispenza (2009), leading author, neuroscientist and speaker who has done extensive research on the impact of meditation on developing new neural pathways in the brain – he advises to 'spend time contemplating who you want to be. The mere process of contemplating who you want to be changes your brain.'

Even when we have a diagnosis there will be times when we can contemplate who we want to be and we can get the support to be those things.

In fact, many people with a diagnosis have become extremely successful, challenging their divergent thinking into creativity, building businesses, thinking outside of the box and bringing an edge to the workplace that other people simply don't have. So it is my belief that yes, your mental health diagnosis can actually give you edge. It takes time, however, and a real feeling of 'training with weights on' to channel your thinking and other symptoms in a direction that can be beneficial to you.

I was speaking to a friend just last week who highlighted their attuned intuition and ability to read people without that person even saying anything. He said he gets it all the time, someone saying how intuitive he is and therefore able to make insightful work decisions and lead his team to success. Knowing that he also has PTSD, I wondered what the line was between that well-honed intuition and the hypervigilance he needed to develop at a younger age due to trauma. We laughed as we discussed how the awful need to learn to keep himself safe has led to an astute ability to be successful in life.

A word on anxiety

Anxiety is seen as the most prevalent mental health challenge in our society, with a host of advice on how to fix or manage it. First of all, let's note the difference between feeling anxious and anxiety disorders – any of us can feel anxious and often that feeling will be connected to doing something outside of our comfort zone. If you're headed to an interview or speaking on stage, feeling anxious is your body's way of telling you to be careful about this new and unfamiliar situation.

On the other hand, there are a variety of anxiety disorders as described by BetterHelp (2022) including generalized anxiety disorder, panic disorder – even obsessive-compulsive disorder (OCD) is viewed as an anxiety disorder. You may have an anxiety disorder if you feel anxious all or most of the time regardless of what is going on around you. It's important to note that you can recover from anxiety disorders and if we come back to the neuroplasticity of the brain there's a lot more that we can do to help this process along than we ever thought possible before.

Anxiety has greatly increased over the past few years and there are a few reasons for this – one is the amount of fear that the media pumps into our nervous system in an always-on society, another is our habits changing due to the amount of time we've spent in isolation, not interacting with simple tasks such as routines around the office or travel. Even now that we're back to a hybrid world, technology is set up to make our lives as stress free as possible, often robbing us of the tiny opportunities to practise bravery. For example, Uber has new 'comfort settings' that can be set prior to taking a journey, where you can decide whether you'd like the driver to engage in conversation or keep to a quiet ride. While you may say this is wonderful as it gives us choice, often where we are given choice to stay safe or be brave we will choose the easier option – the quiet ride – thereby robbing us of a simple opportunity to challenge our anxiety through interacting in a low-risk way.

Due to the prominence of addictive technologies and habits of avoidance, we're often not noticing how we're actually feeling (sometimes we want to run away from our feelings at all costs!). And so our body reacts, even if in reality we are safe and have everything we need around us. Our body wonders if another pandemic is around the corner, if our loved ones are safe, if we'll be able to handle stress at work and ultimately anxious thinking can become a habit, which we perpetuate by tuning into the negative frequencies of the world.

It's worth asking yourself if you are in a habit of being anxious. This can be difficult to assess as often anxiety shows up in physical reactions and they can feel out of our control – however, zoom out on your life again. Were you always anxious? Were there things that happened that slowly edged you into this feeling? Did it build up over time? What are the thoughts or feelings surrounding the anxiety and have outside influences made them feel worse?

Anxiety disorders can often be a result of being in this fixed habit state for too long (maybe due to childhood trauma, learnt behaviour from those around you or, of course, there can be genetic components). However, even then we can take responsibility for our anxiety. That doesn't mean we won't have moments of panic or physical overwhelm but it does mean that we can learn from these moments, proactively get help and learn about how our own anxiety is affecting us – ultimately still asking ourselves what is in our control and what isn't.

Here are a few things you can experiment with to support you on the journey of breaking the habit of anxiety:

1 Assess your lifestyle. This is a really broad view of course, but it is a crucial step to creating the conditions that will support you to manage things. Are you isolating yourself or avoiding certain situations out of fear that your anxiety will show up? While this seems like a good idea in the short term and you certainly have permission to have a consistent schedule, you may also be preventing your brain from learning how to be in new situations. This simply happens when you show up to them. Things like exercise, nutrition, support networks and pressures can all play a part in anxiety so think about what's in your control to slowly change.

2 Get really honest. Get honest about your environment, relationships, job and importantly, your own brain and how its safety mechanism is probably on full blast trying to protect you from literally everything that can be seen as a threat. We don't have to believe everything that we think – we can thank our brain for trying to protect us and reassure ourselves that trying new things will help our brain adapt and develop. This also means being honest with your therapist, doctor or friends and creating networks that support positive accountability rather than circles of misery. This may sound harsh but I'm pretty sure you know what I mean! Saying to a friend 'I'm feeling really anxious but would like to try meeting for a walk' or 'can we speak on the phone for five minutes so I can try to disrupt how I'm feeling?' or 'I want to speak about what's making me anxious for a

few minutes, but after five minutes can you disrupt my thoughts by asking me what I'm grateful for so I don't get stuck there?' – these are all proactive ways to acknowledge how you're feeling, which can also elicit help and support to do something about it.

3 Develop the skill of bravery. Rather than trying so hard to not be anxious or get to a destination where you're totally cured – why not instead flip the narrative and focus on small things that can help you build the skill of bravery. Brave people don't often feel brave, they simply show up despite how they feel. Accept that your body will still feel anxious from time to time – thank it for looking after you and then inform your body and mind that you are safe and will be trying this new thing to show them. These can be the tiniest of things. Speaking to your barista when ordering coffee if you normally wouldn't, going to a class, joining a network at work, walking a different way from your usual route, being honest (see above) are all small ways that we can build the skill of bravery.

From a positive psychology perspective, it's when we focus on what we do want and where we're headed that we let go of the obsession of getting rid of a feeling. The sooner I was honest with myself and others the more I could move forward and anxiety lost its power – this included saying things like 'I'm really anxious today, it's making my hands shake' – the world wouldn't end and my friend wouldn't run and it just started to lose its power.

We are all different. You may need medication, therapy or may have trauma or other elements impacting how you feel. That's OK. Head out into an adventure of discovering who you truly are and what you truly need.

A word on depression

Depression is a term thrown around loosely these days – you've had a tough day at work, you're sooo depressed – we feel tired or low and describe ourselves as depressed – when perhaps we simply haven't slept well, have eaten crap, watched or listened to fear and conflict and our low mood is communicating something to us – our pain and sadness at being in an environment with little physical or emotional nourishment.

Remember depression can be a sign of burnout, it could be linked to grief, to sadness, to a lack of fulfilment, a reaction to being in a toxic environment and certainly a reaction to not living your version of your life – essentially not thinking for yourself.

Think of depression also like a continuum – rarely is it simply a chemical imbalance that is in a fixed state from the moment a person is born – instead it usually starts somewhere. Sadness over time can develop into a more fixed state, which eventually could lead to clinical depression – when the habit of depression is more fixed in the brain.

Johann Hari (2019) says beautifully 'You aren't a machine with broken parts. You are an animal whose needs are not being met'. What if, before we give away our power to the idea of a chemical imbalance and simply accept our state of depressed being, we ask ourselves a few questions and try really hard to create space to think for ourselves:

Which of my needs are not being met?
What do I want?

Do I deserve to get my needs met?

What could I change in my environment?

What is in my control?

How do I want to feel? Who do I want to be? What situation would help me be that person?

Is my environment (work, relationship, isolation, family, technology, addiction) impacting my mental health negatively?

This takes radical honesty and bravery – two skills that can be developed over time!

The two key questions I experimented with the most when I was building my life from rock bottom depression and addiction were: What three things are you grateful for and who do you want to be?

I know gratitude can feel buzzwordy and a bit trite when you're at the bottom of the barrel fighting for each breath, but the science is clear – practising gratitude allows us to develop new neural pathways and get out of the habit of anxious or depressed thinking.

The Science of Gratitude white paper (Allen, 2018) states that there are significant positive impacts to cultivating a mindset of gratitude, including improved psychological well-being, greater life satisfaction, less materialism and being less likely to suffer burnout. It also highlights how gratitude as a practice can sometimes be trite, such as when it's to paper over the toxicity of a situation, or when someone is trying to explain their level of struggle and it's dismissed with 'Oh just be grateful'.

It's important to be balanced in our view and honest about our own state of mind, and experiment with what will be most beneficial to us.

I wasn't grateful for anything back when I was a drunk trying to numb my shame. I was a victim of my past. For me, having a kid young, trauma seeping through my pores, no education or prospects were all reasons to be depressed, and the people I would surround myself with would agree with me, validating my anxious and depressed thinking.

To me, this is a reason to inject positive psychology into our lives (as opposed to toxic positivity). In short, positive psychology is the science of what makes us well rather than focusing on what makes us sick. Toxic positivity is a new term, which describes a dysfunctional approach to emotional management that causes people to simply refuse to acknowledge difficult emotions such as anger or sadness. Instead, we need to ask ourselves what makes us well rather than focusing just on support groups or strategies for when we're unwell.

If we can flip our focus from just sharing how unwell we all are, we might actually have a little bit of energy left to focus on what makes us well and do our best to create environments that help us thrive. This is why in my team at PVL we ask each other questions like 'what's one thing you'll do to invest in yourself today?'

We create positive accountability around asking what's making us thrive, what's in our control, and when the difficult feelings, anxieties or depression are there, we create space for those feelings without trying to fix or numb them.

Having said that, finding the right therapist who really matches you and your thinking can be the most useful thing ever to happen to you. We all need a witness to our story and some education on how our mind works, the patterns that keep us stuck and space that is just about us.

People have come out of therapy with amazing epiphanies! 'Did you know that I don't have to believe my own thoughts?!' – a colleague once said to me. This is a valuable mindset and I was so pleased that they had discovered it.

In a world of information we can access these lessons everywhere. From TikTok to YouTube, to books or speakers, we are in a wonderful information age where we can access learning wherever we are for free, at any time! I've had people tell me the first place they were brave enough to talk about how they truly felt was an online anonymous forum and this slowly led to them building up the courage to tell someone in person and then to get help. When these tools are used for good they can radically change people's lives and lead them on a path to mental health.

Of course, all this information can be overwhelming, can make us focus on the negatives, can be addictive and sometimes be misleading... after a couple hours on YouTube you could decide you have a multitude of physical and mental illnesses that need immediate attention! You can also feel like everyone is getting it right except you, or that the whole world is screwed so what's the point! Your own thinking can get crowded out with every person's perspective or opinion until you close your laptop exhausted and slump into a deep and depressed sleep.

When I realized I had PTSD I read books about it, watched what people said on YouTube and looked through journals of new research on psychedelics and a host of new frontiers for help. I also made the mistake at first of intensely trying to find 'a cure' or a fix for my PTSD, going through a range of emotions during an episode, from vulnerability and fear to hopeless frustration that it would always be this way, to anger and action to try and fix myself. My boyfriend would say 'you're trying to sledge-hammer it again', as I would try three therapies at once and read books obsessively, trying to fight off this most annoying diagnosis. I'd usually exhaust myself and give up, try to live a normal life only for the cycle to start again when I was in a triggered state.

A frustrating and infuriating way to live life!

I realized over time that for me, acceptance was key and that rather than working towards a linear goal of being cured it was more of a cyclical process of improvement. I live with PTSD *and* there are things I can do to live a great life – including channelling some of the energy I would put into trying to cure myself into building a purposeful busi-ness, having an awareness on my lifestyle (food, move-ment, sugar intake, honesty – the basics!) and being really, really straight up with my team at work!

I remember one meeting I had with a few people in my team where I was snappy and short tempered, asking them why they hadn't done this or that – really not the leader I aspire to be! I was agitated and mean and didn't really realize until after the meeting had ended – as soon as I real-ized I messaged the people who had been in the meeting and apologized. I explained how my PTSD was being trig-gered and so my body was in a fear state and my reaction was to attack – it had nothing to do with them – and in our next meeting we spent time repairing and making sure we made the right decisions for the business together.

Of course it helps that we've created a strong founda-tion of psychological safety in our company. We know useful details about each other's mental health, normalize conversations about good mental health and will also openly say if our anxiety, depression, PTSD, etc are acting up. So me apologizing and talking about my mental health didn't feel like it came from left field.

Not only was being honest and letting it go good for my mental health and who I want to be, it had a ripple effect of building trust and safety as a team. If I as the CEO can be that open, even when something has gone wrong, that does more to give the team permission than me telling HR or a team of mental health first aiders to be ready to listen should someone be struggling.

Dr Ardeshir Mehran is an organizational psychologist who has worked in the corporate space for many years. He has a radical perspective on depression as he argues 'You are not depressed, you are unfinished'. He focuses on high achievers, people with ambition and work ethic who are successful and yet will often feel an emptiness and exhaustion. They tell themselves to just keep pushing towards their next goal in order to feel that sense of achievement they've been after their whole lives. Rather than rushing to a diagnosis, Dr Mehran frames these people as unfinished works of art. He highlights how we are a product of our society and environment, our past traumas and future hopes, who get to change things if we want a different life – even if we've been pointing in this same direction for years.

I realize changing your whole life can feel like a privileged thing to say. Not everyone has the resource or means available to make a dramatic shift such as taking a pay cut or pursuing a career that they love. But it is also too easy to become binary in our thinking when it comes to what's possible or not. Fixed belief systems may tell us 'I can't quit my job even if it has a toxic environment' or 'If I leave this job I will be broke and have nothing'.

But there are always more than two choices. It may be a slower process than a dramatic transformation, but it's valuable to explore the grey area and discover how you can make progress within your means.

In summary, depression and anxiety can mean many things. A natural response to pain or needs not being met, learnt behaviour or habit, a genetic or chemical component, being stuck in a shame cycle of addiction and importantly, it could be a sign that you haven't been truly living your life for a very long time. Try to play with what's in your control and what you can experiment with. No fixed outcome, just a game of finding what's in the middle of the choices you think you have and see what you discover.

Therapies and medication

I want to cover some of the key themes that can impact a person's ability to understand themselves and to subsequently take the right sort of action – which will involve thinking for yourself!

The world is saturated with medication, therapists, health coaches, wellness gurus, influencers and advisers.

I realize that many people don't have access to personal therapists or coaches. It's a real privilege to access psychological support through your country's health service, insurance or even company benefits, or to have the financial resources to get this support yourself. Even when people have access though, they often won't use it – this is due to several factors including fear, shame and stigma – hoping that if they just soldier on the niggling issue will just go away.

Accessing support through work brings up all sorts of challenges – fear that the support isn't confidential (even though you've been told it is), not understanding the process, barriers to entry such as calling a helpline and being asked for personal information, and fear that getting help will be like opening Pandora's box! You know you've been storing stuff up for months, years, decades – maybe your whole life – so there's much uncertainty that comes with starting to talk.

But let's say you get through the first barrier of deciding to get support as well as being able to access it – you're then met with a minefield of types of therapies, types of medications and often different professionals or self-proclaimed influencers saying different things. When you're distressed or in crisis this landscape of choice can feel even more overwhelming and it can be easy to give away our agency to the first professional or influencer we come across. They sound so smart and knowledgeable and we're in pain and just want answers so follow whatever they say – perhaps they suggest going over your story, uncovering trauma or being assessed for a few months, perhaps there's a suggestion of medication or of a support group, online resources, etc.

I remember once being so overwhelmed with my PTSD symptoms that I researched a procedure called stellate ganglion block (SGB), which is essentially injecting a local anaesthetic into the stellate ganglion nerves in your neck, which I would have paid for privately and which may or may not have had any benefit at all. My boyfriend wisely advised me to wait, perhaps until I was out of crisis, to decide if such a drastic procedure was right for me.

I'm sure even this procedure is the right thing for some people but the reality for me was that I wasn't thinking for myself – I was scared, reactive and wanting to fix what I was going through in as easy a way as possible! The idea of a shot to the neck taking away this torment sounded like just the quick fix I was after in that moment.

Which brings me on to medication. I'm all for the right medication matched to the right challenge and finding the right medication has radically changed so many people's lives for the better – allowing them to breathe and *widen the window*, as Elizabeth Stanley PhD describes in her book of the same name (2021). It can just take the edge off, calm the nervous system and allow us to do the work that previously wasn't possible – which can include being able to sit with our feelings or attend therapy.

I remember when I was deeply in addiction and was depressed, I went to my doctor to tell them about my low mood. As all alcoholics know, we will first look to everything else to fix before we look at alcohol and our own behaviour and taking responsibility for our lives – and I mean everything! So I told an older male doctor of my depression. He picked up a form, some sort of list of questions, and began asking and ticking things off, with zero eye-contact, not enquiring about the context of what was going on for me.

The questions must have included how long I had felt that way, maybe a suicide or risk question, but ultimately, no matter what the questions were, there was no connection between me and this doctor. I didn't feel listened to so when he tossed me a prescription for Prozac I left it in a drawer and didn't feel comfortable starting it.

I was slowly starting to learn to think for myself.

I didn't just leave the situation, I called up the reception and asked if it was possible to see a different doctor. These days many medical practices in the UK also have a mental health nurse or someone with just a little bit more training in this area – so always ask if that's the case! This second doctor listened with empathy and kindness, heard my worries about Prozac and gave me a prescription for a much lower dose SSRI to get me started.

If something doesn't feel right, it's OK to ask for a second opinion.

Not that these antidepressants worked for me, because depression wasn't really my issue. Alcohol addiction, trauma and subsequent PTSD symptoms were. I also wasn't supposed to drink while on the meds but I would drink anyway and would get violently sick, leading me to stop the medication but not the booze (obviously).

Medication can be the best thing that's ever happened to someone – allowing them to re-engage with the world, or to reconnect with family and friends. Where there is a chemical imbalance, some people may need this support for their mental health for the rest of their lives.

What we forget though is that no one thing is THE solution. Each thing is a piece of your personal puzzle that can change over time but, crucially, that needs other pieces in order to ensure that you can improve your mental health and thrive.

So ask yourself:

Does this advice feel right for me?
What assumptions am I making about this option?
Do I feel listened to by this doctor or therapist – does their opinion make sense to me and the wider context of my life, body and experience?
Do I have a trusted friend I can sense check things with?
Am I getting stuck in conditioned patterns of behaviour or am I thinking for myself?

Nobody knows you better than you!

Of course there are times when you may need backup. If you're in a crisis, you may need someone to think for you for a little while – to take the pressure off, so you can just lay back and get well and that's OK! And then you'll re-emerge into awareness and be able to ask yourself, what part can I play in my care plan, what do I need to say, what do I want to experiment with and who do I want to be?

While I haven't been able to cover the entire scope of mental illness, I hope this chapter has given you a few key principles and ideas to consider if you're struggling with burnout, anxiety or depression. Of course there are lots of other mental illnesses that may be affecting you but in summary, I believe a few key principles apply.

A diagnosis is not a sentence. It's information about what your body and mind need. Learn about it and then connect these ideas to your own body and try them on for size.

What we think we know about our mind isn't fixed. Advances in neuroscience are giving us new information every day so see hope – there is more that we are able to do to change things than we ever thought before!

No matter who tells you what's going on for you, be it a health professional or therapist, do your own research too, get second opinions and take on an attitude of experimenting with what works for you. Even though you can't always believe your thoughts, you can learn to emotionally regulate, and as Dr Caroline Leaf puts it 'clean up your mental mess' (2021).

In the next chapter I'm going to talk about maintaining good mental health as a lifetime practice. Creating uplifting and healthy habits is critical to sustaining long-term success so follow me for the next stage of our journey.

CHAPTER FIVE

Maintenance, attitude and living a good life now

For many of us, we're not in crisis – or at least not if we're managing our mental health with the right level of support. Crisis can often make us realize the importance of investing in our well-being in order to sustain success long term.

People who are maintaining good mental health proactively are often the ones who've experienced full-blown burnout, a physical illness caused by stress, rock bottom points due to addiction or crisis due to a mental health diagnosis. We've learnt the hard way that our health is the most important thing we have! Without health we cannot achieve any form of success, impact or legacy.

How many times have you felt brain fog creep in, nervous system trembles, back pain, relentless headaches, poor sleep, heart palpitations or a variety of other early-warning signs and ignored them in order to just do one more job or achieve one more goal.

We tell ourselves it won't get that bad and we listen to the influencers who tell us to just visualize our goal, do the work and eventually we will achieve ultimate success. Except once we achieve one goal we firmly set our sights on the next one and the next and the next, so we never actually get to a place of arrival, which means success is always transient and our body just has to keep going no matter the cost!

Not to mention how the world of work is changing! Working from home, hybrid work, balancing new priorities, portfolio careers, families, older relatives, bereavement, conspiracy theories and fear are all jacked up more than they ever were before!

So how are we meant to listen to our bodies and true thoughts when everything around us is confusing and adding noise to our internal frequency? How do we evolve what success means and our ways of getting there, along with our changing times? How do we maintain optimum well-being to sustain success (whatever that means to you).

Firstly, it's taking time to zoom out of our lives again. Remember the Google Maps imagery of your life? First see who you are in the centre of things, experiencing those annoying feelings that you keep trying to squash, numb or avoid and then zoom out further until you see your whole life map. Your work, family, context, system, routines, habits and thinking. Your thinking and actions have set up that whole life for you! Take a minute to reflect on your part in taking your life to this exact wondrous point!

And I say that knowing full well that you may have had trauma like me or a less than ideal past, without the optimum emotional support, which has influenced your actions and definitely stacked up to impact your mental health. Feeling like a victim of our circumstance or even of our poor mental health doesn't help us take radical responsibility and take the steps necessary to invest in our well-being – in fact it does the opposite! It keeps us running in one race, one line, one direction – one that we may not even have ownership of – wondering why achievement of things, people and status just isn't giving us what we thought it would. In fact, we may even feel worse than before we had all those pressures and achievements!

There are amazing resources out there that can help teach us to be in the present, to actually see the small things again, to notice what's around us, to appreciate who we are and what we can become. From Buddhist teachings to mindfulness practices, yoga, gratitude, journalling, nature – whatever works for you.

The responsibility I'm talking about in maintaining good mental health includes a few things:

- **Reflect:** Reflecting on where you are and taking radical responsibility for your part in it.
- **Educate:** Educate yourself on the ways of your mind and body – rather than mindlessly scrolling on any given topic – get recommendations from people, consciously look for ideas that fit for you, and just so you're aware, therapy or coaching count as education too! Sometimes what we need is a safe space to hear our own ideas out loud so that we can make sense of them!

- **Experiment:** Just as if you were a marketing expert and needed to test strategies before picking one route to market, or a scientist trying a range of variables before coming to a hypothesis, the same goes for your well-being and mental health maintenance! This can be done with lightness and humour and doesn't have to be 'sledgehammering it' as I can be guilty of. It's a journey not a destination – how can you create an environment that enables more chances for joy! Joy and happiness are transient emotions just like sadness and anger – emotions don't generally stay static, they change and evolve and that's OK. To be human is to feel. If you feel a lot of things, that doesn't mean you're mentally ill, it often means your body is giving you information – maybe it's a lot of overwhelming information at once because you're unpractised at listening to your body – that's OK! That's the start of learning to understand what you truly need and moving into a mentally healthy place where you can sustain and enjoy success long term.

Work–life balance and evolving our daily practices

Our world is more sedentary than ever. According to GWI, in 2022 the average amount of daily screen time for adults in the UK was 6 hours and 12 minutes, with adults in the US spending 7 hours and 4 minutes on average in front of a screen (Kemp, 2022). That's not only a lot of screen time, it's also a lot of sitting! While more people are using standing desks or integrating walking meetings, there is conflicting evidence on how much benefit there is from standing in one place, and with meeting culture, differing time zones meaning early or late starts, we simply aren't moving as much as is healthy!

When we're tired and burnt out it's also harder to make healthy choices when it comes to nutrition, movement or socializing. Unhealthy habits begin to creep in as we try to avoid, escape or numb the feeling inside us that something just isn't quite right. That we're not doing our thinking, that we're on a path we're not sure we like any more, that our health is suffering, we're not as productive, focused or mission driven as we once thought and the idea of success is making us compare, feel flawed or frustrated.

But we ignore all that and keep pushing forward. If we just hustle hard enough we will achieve our goals – not questioning what might be on the other side of that achievement – and what it will truly cost once we achieve it.

There are a few things that are crucial to evolving our working practices.

Movement! How can we evolve our day to incorporate as much movement and energy-boosting activity as possible? How can we bravely do things differently? I've had meetings with very important people and asked if we could do an audio call so that we could walk and talk. Across the board people will reply with 'What a great idea! I hadn't thought of doing this during my day' or 'It's true, I could walk most of the day if I wanted to'.

In my team every person takes responsibility for their own mental health, which includes letting the team know what they need that day to invest in themselves. Today I'm going to stay off camera so I can walk and talk, can we cancel a meeting or make sure flexi work actually means flexible work – that means we're looking for mission-driven outputs and don't mind how or when exactly you get those things done! We want you to take responsibility for your health as much as you take responsibility for your tasks – that's on you – but it's my responsibility as an employer to allow you to do that.

Trauma therapies these days are all about movement. Somatic therapies, noticing that stress, trauma and burn-out are stuck in our body not our mind. When we release our body and 'complete our stress cycle' (Nagoski and Nagoski, 2020) we are helping our mind at the same time! People seem to forget that our body is attached to our head! They also don't realize that regurgitating the same story about your toxic boss over and over doesn't actually prevent burnout – it may even keep you stuck in the tunnel of stress longer and perpetuate the cycle. Movement allows you to release the stress from your body.

So first, see how you can radically incorporate move-ment into your day and then get brave enough to tell others so you can influence change – just you on your own, you can make a difference!

Let's be clear, some of the most successful people I know do both! They take up high-intensity exercise (boxing, CrossFit, HIIT, etc), as they know that to not do it means they will be snappy, unfocused or make poor decisions – essentially they won't be able to perform at their optimum best! Their body helps their mind achieve greatness!

The 'Five ways to well-being' researched by the New Economics Foundation (Aked et al, 2008) gives a great baseline for maintaining good mental health – and we need the follow-up question of how we evolve these practices into a changing world:

- Be active – movement in your working day
- Connect – in a hybrid world
- Give back – listen and show empathy for others – create a thinking space for them
- Keep learning – get curious, experiment with new ways of working
- Take notice – smell the roses, as they say. Look at this wonderful life that you lead!

Taking responsibility for your mental health, which will enable your version of success, includes experimenting with all of these ways and finding out what you want to dial up in your life – and crucially, how to create space in order to do so!

Who are the connections in your life? Who are you surrounding yourself with and listening to? What influences are you allowing in your life and is there some conscious thought that can be put into this? A simple assessment is asking yourself 'does this person give me energy or drain it?' But of course, if a friend is struggling with their mental health it may feel a bit draining for a while; that may just mean you need boundaries around the level of support you can give and can trust that they have their own agency and support networks to get them through. More on supporting others in the next chapter!

Continuing to learn and develop yourself is good for your mental health! Just remember to decide for yourself which bits apply to you and which bits you will hold on to lightly. You don't need to believe everything you read – even when it comes to goals, success or mental health – including this book!

Taking notice is really about embracing where you are right now! Your mind, your body, your life is a gift and life has the potential for beauty, connection and growth – notice it! The thing is, as Dr Brené Brown (2022) says:

> Joy is vulnerable.
> We're afraid to lean into joy because something might rip it away and we'll get sucker punched by disappointment or pain.

Sometimes noticing where you are and feeling the joy of life as a gift opens up the other feelings too. When I am open to love I am also open to pain – not just the pain of potential loss right here and now, but all the unprocessed pain bubbling up from my past. Noticing what we feel and being open to good emotions is a brave act in a world mired by negativity and struggle.

When was the last time you said to someone at work (or anywhere): what's one thing that's amazing about your life right now? What's one thing you're grateful for? What does love feel like for you? What's the last moment of joy that you felt?

We don't say these things. We're embarrassed to talk about the good stuff! People are struggling everywhere and we tell ourselves we should show solidarity and struggle alongside them – but what happened to being a light! What happened to showing a different way? When did it stop being OK to talk about the good stuff?

Victor Frankl gives us clear ideas for how we can shift our perspective no matter what we're going through – he says 'between stimulus and response there is a space. In that space is our power to choose our own response. In our response lies our growth and freedom'.

In a world of propaganda, death, trauma and noise, Victor Frankl figured out how to think for himself and went on not only to survive where others did not, but to go on to develop a psychological approach called logotherapy, which posits that the primary motivational force of an individual is to find meaning in life. Even in the small things.

One of the greatest things that can give us meaning is giving back to others. This means taking a break from our own thinking and instead putting our focus on someone else. Being there for others can promote gratitude, connection and take us out of our comfort zone – all elements that support a mentally healthy life.

In the next chapter I want to focus on how to support others in a way that enhances your mental health rather than leading to empathy fatigue or burnout. If Covid-19 lockdowns taught us anything it's that we need each other in order to counter loneliness, enhance a feeling of belonging and foster good mental health, and there's so many of us that truly enjoy being there for others. The next chapter highlights the benefits and pitfalls and gives you some key principles to hold in mind in your role as helper.

CHAPTER SIX

Supporting others

How we show up in the world in our behaviours, at work and in our circles of friends, has more influence than us advising, telling or trying to influence their behaviour.

Think about your friend struggling with depression. They tell you about some trauma they suffered, grief they are feeling or pain they are experiencing, and you begin telling them in great detail how they should follow a particular nutrition plan or framework, or *just* go outside. Not only does this person ignore your advice (even if it was sound), instead they feel mildly infuriated, misunderstood and like no one will ever, and I mean EVER, understand them!

They may begin pushing people away or isolating further, as every time they say what they're struggling with, someone has a new article they've read, YouTube video they've watched or supplement they've taken that they definitely, definitely should try. Said isolation can make them feel worse, because remember, we do need healthy connection, and eventually they can spiral into a worse place than before.

With the best intention in the world, you have not helped – and you may even have made things worse – again, with the best intention.

Here are a few steps to consider when wanting to support a friend or colleague who may be struggling:

1 Listen and acknowledge what you've heard
2 Connect to what they've been through personally by offering something of yourself
3 Turn back to them – really listen
4 Empower personal agency (find out what works for them and provide support for them to do that one small thing)

Allow me to explain…

Step 1: Listen and acknowledge what you've heard

I recently watched the Netflix documentary *Stutz*, where the actor Jonah Hill interviews his therapist in order to get his proactive therapy tools to the masses. He says something interesting, which I think many people may relate to – we just want our friends to listen and they offer us unsolicited advice, and we want our therapist to give us advice and they just listen – a useful comment on what we as friends could do better by just listening, as well as some insight into how the therapy world needs to continue to evolve.

What people need is space to be heard. They need to be seen, valued and understood. If you want to help – shut the hell up. Listen with your eyes, with your body language and with your intention. In an age of distraction this is actually harder than it sounds!

Try it sometime… with a friend, a partner or colleague. Listen to their story, make sure your phone is out of arm's reach and simply give them your full attention. See how long you can last for!

It seems that our attention spans are shortening year by year. We even tend to do two things at once, such as watching TV while working on our laptop, reading a book while checking our Instagram feed. It's getting harder to read a full book from cover to cover, with some people stating they simply don't read books any more, trading them in for TikTok shorts.

I see *focus* as the new frontier of work! The superpower of productivity! Having the capacity to ignore the pings of your phone and communicate boundaries to those around you will be the ninja employee of the future – beyond technological advances and with the rise of remote working, we'll be measured more on focused output rather than hours on the job – people who have mastered this skill (as well as skills such as emotional intelligence and communication) will have the edge in the job market.

Think of the last meeting you were in or business lunch you had, did you or the other person plant your phone face up in the middle of the table, priming it to distract you at any given time? It's become normalized to say 'oh I'm sorry, just a minute, I have to take this' no matter what point of the conversation you're at or how unimportant the call is.

So the first skill in being able to support others effectively is to manage your distractions and get good at giving attention.

There's the practical boundary we can set of leaving our phone in a pocket or bag or only answering if we've been waiting for something urgent and preparing the person we're with for that possibility. This is part of leading by example. 'Let me turn my phone off so I can really listen to what's going on for you' is a powerful thing to say and do in this day and age.

The skill here is to simply practise listening without interruption. To sit with the strangeness of silence, showing curiosity in your face as you encourage the person to tell you more. The second part of this skill is to acknowledge the feeling that person is communicating. Not the facts, or even the story, as you have no basis on which to comment on that – instead, comment on the emotion.

'That sounds really hard', 'that sounds really overwhelming' or 'I'm so sorry it's such an intense time for you' are all examples of acknowledging what you've heard.

We're often most nervous of acknowledging the emotion in the situation and so we soldier on, advising on the facts – making the person feel the opposite of seen, heard and valued.

'Our society is terrified of tears and anger and fear', says Nancy Klein (2002) in her revolutionary book *Time to Think*. 'We have mixed up the release of pain with the cause of pain. Stop crying and you'll stop hurting. Stop showing your anger and you'll stop being angry. Stop shaking and you'll stop being afraid. Just stop it'.

Creating space for someone to think and feel is the most powerful gift we can give them and we don't actually have to be a professional to do this. Yes, it is a skill that can be developed, but each and every one of us can develop it through reading and practice. Let go of the need to speak or find a solution when someone else is telling you about their struggle. Instead, practise being curious. Even if you know the headline of what someone might be going through – like depression or anxiety, but also just life circumstances like divorce or bereavement – you still don't know what *they* are going through; you don't know what it's like for them!

Step 2: Connect to what they've been through personally by offering something of yourself

It can be tempting to instantly connect with someone's experiences and link them to your own – but this just leads to shifting the focus on yourself. This doesn't mean you can't show up vulnerably yourself but there's an art to showing you understand by putting a bit of yourself in the mix and then transitioning the conversation back to them – inviting them to tell you more. A useful approach to enhance connection while also being supportive is 'that sounds like a big transition' (acknowledge what you know), 'I actually went through a divorce myself a few years back' (connection personally), 'I'm curious, what's it like for you?' (turn it back over to the individual and listen).

This works with mental health issues too. For example, 'That sounds like a lot, I had a friend who experienced depression, but I know everyone can experience it differently, what's it like for you?'

There is a clear difference between diverting the conversation due to your discomfort around the subject-matter and actually supporting and engaging with the other person's experience. So showing something of yourself is useful because it makes you human and helps somebody feel safe in sharing more.

Of course, if they ask you 'how did you get through that time?' that's giving you permission to continue a little more, perhaps by saying 'well, to be honest, I had to get some counselling' or 'I tried medication/meditation' – whatever is true for you, but then crucially, keep Step 3 in mind:

Step 3: Turn back to them, really listen

Say something like 'so those are the things that helped me, but I know that everyone is different and your experience has so many things I don't know about. What kind of things have you tried already?'

What you've done there is bring something of yourself, checked for permission to add more and then ensured you've brought the space back to them. Remember, they are the one who needs help right now, you have gotten through something and are on the other side (well done!).

People often give hints that they want to be heard but then deflect back to you to test if you're really a trustworthy person who values them and wants to give them the space they are desperate for.

So listen. Don't be afraid of emotion, that can just be relief, release and part of being in a shared space where they aren't judged and it's OK to talk. And then there's what I call encouraging personal accountability or agency when appropriate. That leads us on to:

Step 4: Empower personal agency

Empowering personal agency is about knowing that even if you've seen something before or if you have been through something similar, you've read some books on the topic or even if you're a manager or professional, the person you're trying to support will always know more about themselves than you do.

They are living in their body, experiencing their thoughts and have tried a variety of things before.

Empowering personal agency is about calling on their own experiences and strengths and encouraging them to take action in a way that they see is possible – with a bit of challenge from you of course!

If it's someone in my team for example, a way to empower personal agency is, after following the other steps above, asking a version of the questions below:

What's one thing you can do to invest in yourself – even if it's really small?

When you felt better, were there any things you were doing that were helping?

How can we be accountable as a team to help us feel better at work?

Showing through your behaviours is crucial, being brave enough to listen and trust that they know more than they let on ensures a strengths-based approach and enhances that feeling of backup and community that can support any person to do the things to create change.

Of course, there are some basic principles that can help us all invest in our well-being: physical exercise, seeing a doctor, calling a helpline or following the framework you read about in an article that you've been dying to tell them about this whole time *could* help – but it won't if it's not delivered in the right way and at the right time. Sometimes it's just not the right time. Sometimes you just do Step 1 – that's all – you listen and acknowledge what they're going through. You don't have to achieve all these steps in one sitting, they can show up over days, months or years of supporting someone.

Remember you can influence through your actions too – 'I'm going for a walk during my lunch break, want to come?' is very different from 'I really think it would help if you went for a walk'.

So, practise the steps and see what your personal stretch-zone is – notice when your friends try to help but don't do these steps, notice how you tend to help but where you may fall flat – and if you're in therapy by all means, find a therapist who will offer you some tools to practise, not just sit there and listen.

Once again, in summary:

1 Listen and acknowledge what you've heard
2 Connect to what they've been through personally by offering something of yourself
3 Turn back to them – really listen
4 Empower personal agency (find out what works for them and provide support for them to do that one small thing)

Creating safe spaces at work

I've given some thoughts on creating a safe space with a person and setting the conditions for that to happen. Those steps can apply with friends, family or at work – however, how do we do this in offices or remotely? Is it really possible to listen at work?

First, these skills are great for business too. Really listening and giving attention enhances creativity, boosts confidence and fosters team cohesion and a sense of belonging. It doesn't have to take hours either! Just five minutes without distraction, truly listening and giving attention to someone can build trust over time.

Some of us are used to the quiet of our home offices now and so coming into the office a few days a week can bring about sensory overload and a real challenge in reducing distraction. Many organizations are back in their offices but still on Teams meetings anyway, to be inclusive of people at home – which can often mean we need to be more proactive about talking to people in real life at work.

It is possible to create a safe space on a video call, an old-school telephone call, in-person at work or even in a message. The principles still apply. Sure it might not be appropriate to go into their life story or they may not be comfortable telling you about the full struggle, but you are planting the seeds of helping them feel heard, seen and valued. This builds psychological safety so when there is space, the foundation has already been set.

Newer office spaces are set up with well-being in mind. Little corners with sofas, secluded meeting rooms or café areas can all work for giving attention to others – you may just have to work a little bit harder at not getting distracted. Another great way to connect if you have the option available is to go for coffee around the corner from the office, have a walking meeting or, as I do with my team, who are fully remote, check in on each other from time to time while walking and on your phone. This brings a more informal air to the call and if you're a leader or manager you can set the scene or expectations.

For example, I might say 'I'd really like to spend the first bit of this call just seeing how you are and then a bit later we can get into any tasks or questions.' This relieves anxiety as people know what to expect and can breathe and behave accordingly.

How to signpost effectively

Lots of mental health training at work focuses on signposting. They remind us to the point of nervousness that we are NOT professionals and therefore should NOT touch topics we know nothing about. While I agree that there will be some things that need professional support, and we certainly shouldn't advise on someone's mental illness, I think this fear is heightened in places like the US that have a highly litigious culture and it also taps into the fears I mentioned previously. I see so many organizations afraid to say anything at work for fear that saying the wrong thing will land them in some kind of trouble. While I understand that we should be thoughtful and careful, this is a real shame.

So we touch mental illness with a 10-foot pole and signpost people to a professional: occupational health, an EAP helpline, human resources or perhaps a self-help app.

While I understand that often this is because we simply want the best for people and don't want to get things wrong, we can often perpetuate stigma by sending the message that the individual is too much, a risk of some kind and thereby must swiftly be sent over *there* where they can be professionally dealt with. Does that person access those services? In most cases probably not. They came to you because they trust you and they were finally brave enough to say something and while I know many of you are amazing empathetic listeners, ultimately, we often send them away.

Signposting is about letting people know about services that are available in language that is accessible and welcoming. Many people have no idea what benefits or support is on offer in their workplace so there is definitely a place for mentioning these and even better, if you've used them, talk about your experience to help reassure them about the process.

In order to create a mentally healthy culture, however, we cannot just outsource mental health to someone else – we must each take responsibility for our culture ourselves and do our part in normalizing conversations about mental health throughout our working day. If you've been reading previous chapters, this doesn't just mean talking about the struggle, it means challenging each other to take personal agency for our lifestyles and working practices – and importantly, talking about it.

Make sure you're abreast of what's on offer and make sure you access the support yourself when useful – and then follow the steps of listening and attention first. You don't have to know the answers or be able to fix things (a natural habit to lean into, especially in the workplace where fixing things may be part of your normal job); instead, asking curious questions and wondering at things they've done already or would like to try to support them creates space for them to do their own thinking.

And if there's something way out of your league that they're going through – be honest, for example: 'I don't know much about depression to be honest but I'm happy to listen and support where I can. Did you know we also have XYZ resource that's totally free? I used it once myself (if this is true) and I felt this bit was really useful – do you know the number? If you're interested, I've got it right here in my phone and can share it with you.' Next time you meet, it's also OK to say, 'hey were you able to find time to get some support? No worries if not, I was just curious'. This allows the person to feel remembered and it's up to them what they say but you have planted another seed of trust, which builds psychological safety.

And of course this brings us to telling our stories. Many passionate people who have the empathy and capability to listen have a personal story themselves about their own struggle – burnout, diagnosis, addiction, bereavement and finding ways to manage our own success are powerful drivers that help us want to help others. This is beautiful and the world gets changed by activists who believe deeply in what they are talking about. However, there are a few principles I've learnt along the way that can help you judge when this is appropriate and know how to look after yourself if you experience what Dr Brené Brown coined 'a vulnerability hangover'.

How to tell your story at work

Telling our stories can be hard.

Knowing when to tell our stories is equally important and recognizing our need to look after ourselves after telling our stories can feel like a minefield.

Remember I never used to tell my backstory – if I did it was a version that only elicited curiosity and a feeling of specialness. I just said that my parents travelled a lot. Sometimes I said they were missionaries, which at least gave people some sense of a framework. If I tested out the word cult (which I first had to admit to myself) people immediately thought of horrific tragedies such as the Jonestown Massacre in 1978 or Heaven's Gate in 1997. None of this captures my experience so I avoided saying too much. Whatever your background or expertise, it's inevitable that people will jump to conclusions based upon their own perspective. This makes it even more important to learn about ourselves, practice bravery and nurture support networks around us.

I now speak on stages globally telling my story in front of thousands of people and I hope, as you've heard some of my story in this book, that there may be one small thing from my story that can impact yours positively. It's not just about taking specific insights from our stories but the process of telling them that empowers us and connects us as people. This can be powerful and useful. When we tell our stories of diversity, of gender, of race, of neurodivergence and mental illness – we realize that we all are human. We all have a story.

This radically helped my victim narrative. If I was brave enough to tell my story, then others would feel comfortable telling theirs. This wasn't the intention; it was the by-product. I simply couldn't live with a mask on any more – I knew it would kill me – so rather than being brave, I started telling my story simply to survive. And I discovered something wonderful, everyone had a story!

Some were much worse than mine, others were lighter but they all held pain, human suffering, resilience and bravery. I was not alone.

We tell our stories at work so that we can remind ourselves that we're not just employees, titles and targets. We are in fact humans with lives, neuroses, families, challenges and the one thing that ties us all together – how short life is and that we want to survive and maybe even find a way to thrive – even at work!

So tell your story. Start small, build from there and practise courage. This is what will help us find our version of success – seeing that people aren't their Instagram profiles or their LinkedIn bio's – people deal with stress, trauma and struggle every day and yet they show up at life – and often they're even happy! It's a beautiful tribe to be part of!

I'm not encouraging everyone to pursue a career in public speaking of course; being open and brave can be with family, a friend, a therapist or colleague. It's about owning your story and having a witness.

When we do tell our stories, especially at first, there can be a comedown afterwards. Dr Brené Brown coined the phrase 'vulnerability hangover' (TED, 2010), which I think fits well here. She describes it as the 'gut-wrenching feeling of shame and fear that pops right after we undertake an emotional risk'. I'm sure many of you have experienced this before. I took up therapy again a few months ago after a long hiatus, and for three days afterwards I was intensely irritable and angry – emotions that I'd packed away nicely were bubbling to the surface and the shame that I was even feeling these things put me into that gut-wrenching vulnerability hangover place.

The difference now from before is that I have a word for it and I can understand my experience and know that it will pass. It's just cause and effect. I can tell my partner or my team that I'm having a vulnerability hangover and it just needs a day or three to shake out of my system. If you have the right people in your life they will commend you for your effort and bravery and ask if there's anything they can do to help.

Of course sometimes we need to say no to telling our stories. I've seen people who've taken on the diversity and inclusion agenda, sometimes nominated by someone else simply because of their race, gender or other diversity to be the voice of the entire workplace on this topic. Some people love this role and for some people it's assumed that they want to take on their entire demographic's struggle – and people want emotion and fire and passion so they want the story again and again. And you're spent, burnt out, want to live your life rather than bear the weight and responsibility of everyone's struggle.

Perhaps you've struggled with your mental health and are open about it at work and every awareness day or well-being initiative you're asked to tell your story. You're passionate and you want to help but every time you have to numb out just a little more, you need time to recover or your nervous system is triggered into a state of fight, flight or freeze. This is where self-awareness is key! Where are you at right now? Do you want to take on the role of activist in your company? Do you want to show through your behaviour that we can invest in ourselves and talk openly about our stories, but also our recovery and our changing well-being needs? Or do you want instead to tell your story at home, to a therapist or, like me, start with a support group or even an online forum. At different times in your life you may want different things.

Remember to think for yourself and listen to your body.

Remember that you are strong enough to push a little outside your comfort zone every time and you're also allowed to say no.

Learning what your boundaries are is a crucial part of maintaining good mental health, creating an impact in the world and supporting others effectively. It's OK to say 'no I'm unable to do that right now'. It's OK to say 'no I can't attend that meeting, is there another way I can help solve the problem?' It's OK to say 'no I can't tell my story this time, let's see if some other people would like to do it'. Or 'I need to take a break from being a mental health champion or a diversity and inclusion ally as I need to prioritize my own mental health'.

It's OK to say no. In fact, it's essential to success.

You may need to say no to a hundred things to have the opportunity to say yes to that one beautiful mission.

Think of an athlete who is training for the 100-metre sprint. They have a coach, nutrition and sleep plan, times when they're in recovery and times when they're hitting it hard. They have to say no to that night out in order to say yes to training and winning their race. They even have to say no to competing in other sports because their specific skill is such a nuanced art that in order to be the best they have to double down on that one thing.

What's the thing you really want?

Not what you should do or think you need to do or what everyone else is telling you to do. That thing that's still a flicker of a flame in your belly that feels scary and personal and maybe even secret – that thing!

If you're going to double down on that one thing and see if it's possible in this one tiny precious life – what else do you need to say no to?

There are parts of my story I never tell on stage. They're just too raw or difficult to talk about – but there are other parts of my story I thought I would never talk about but now I do confidently and it brings power to my message. The important thing is not to feel pressured by what anyone else is asking you to do but instead, in small ways, with the right people, push that little bit out of your comfort zone and ask yourself, what's the impact I want to create in the world? The story that helps you do that is the story to tell.

But you have to start small. It might be the tearful telling in therapy or the stunted story in front of a friend. That's the starting point. Well done!

The next chapter is for those of you who want to go deeper into telling your stories, leading by example and creating change as an internal activist at work! Let's discuss how to create a movement for change in your workplace!

CHAPTER SEVEN

Internal activism and changing the world of work

Activism is all about campaigning for change.
This is what I do every day: teaching, inspiring and advising on how to change our worlds of work for the better! To have a strategic approach that is about how we show up every day, our working practices with the hope of not only preventing despair, suicide and burnout but making work good for our mental health! A place where we truly understand that success isn't just numbers, success is creating environments that sustain our ability to do creative work and will allow us to innovate within our industries and adapt our workplaces for the future. It's the people that will help us do that and here are a few things

to consider when on the journey of creating a mentally healthy culture.

Change takes time.

Sometimes it feels impossible. Sometimes change starts out of crisis. The number of companies that have come to me because there's been a suicide and now they think they should do something is staggering. I don't advocate for crisis as the reason for change, this should only be a last resort, but sometimes it is the only thing that can wake leadership up to realizing that there is a real challenge with their people and that they need to take action now.

Sometimes change will not happen in your lifetime and if your work environment negatively impacts your road to success, it may be time to cut your losses. Remember, listen to your own voice, no one else, on that.

So it's important to know what you can do to help create change and what challenges can only be tackled from a systemic perspective and are the responsibility of leadership.

A few key themes to consider

When we focus on the crisis end of the mental health continuum our engagement is often lower than we'd like. By which I mean, if all of your training, initiatives and events focus on learning about the signs and symptoms of poor mental health, well then we often end up like meerkats peeking over the dunes on the lookout for everything that is wrong with the world.

This is the opposite of a psychologically positive approach. An approach that is visionary and thinking about what a mentally healthy culture might look like and what the objectives are that you'll need to put in place to get you there. Shawn Achor (TED, 2012) describes the problem so well in his TED talk titled 'The happy secret to better work' – talking through a wellness week planned at a school. He hilariously describes the ailment they will visit each week day, including self-harm, bullying and violence, eating disorders, etc. Listening thoughtfully he comes back to them, saying 'that's not a wellness week, that's a sickness week'.

How many of our mental health allies and initiatives are focused on sickness rather than wellness? We think about driving ourselves to success but we don't really think about what success means for us individually or even as a business when it comes to the culture we want to create. This applies to inclusion and all types of causes internal activism could be promoting. Do we ask ourselves what a truly inclusive workplace would look like, right through to the detail of behaviours, leadership, policies, working culture and business goals? Do we ask ourselves what a mentally healthy culture would even look like so we know where we're headed and what our goal is rather than simply putting in benefits and helplines to manage the people, sidelining us from what we perceive to be the only success goals – profit, speed and growth?

I like to put in an 80/20 rule here and I use this when building a mental health strategy for a company. We will audit their intranet, posters, initiatives, language, ally networks, data, surveys, etc and will advise that 80 per cent of what they put out there should focus on good mental health and where they want to be headed, while of course 20 per cent can still be 'when you're struggling, here is the support'.

We want to normalize conversations about thriving. How are we working? How can we build trust and psychological safety together? How can we create the environments that help our people thrive and feel successful – fulfilled in their work but also in their whole life. So when my team talks about mental health our voices don't automatically do a downward turn as if expecting the answer to be negative. When people tell us they're struggling we don't automatically tell them to take time off work – we collaborate on what they think will be useful. Remember, a mentally healthy culture can be a protective factor where someone wants to stay – not something they have to leave to recover from.

You're not going to be able to properly lead by example unless you practise being open and uplifting! The best place to start practising is with your network of other passionate people. Ask yourselves what you want to get out of the group, your vision for yourselves, the ripple effect you can each create and the vision for mental health at your organization. We have moved way beyond just tackling stigma! That cannot be your only objective. Instead, ask yourselves what does moving past reducing stigma mean and how will you do it?

The way to start is by normalizing the conversation about mental health and reframing what it takes to sustain success in your daily actions and conversations.

It's living a lifestyle that invests in your long-term success by learning, connecting, giving back, staying present and moving your body! It's finding ways within the working day to ensure these elements can be met. It takes bravery to say 'do you mind doing a walk-and-talk meeting? It's so good for my mental health when I can move more during the day'. When someone asks how you are or how was your weekend, educate people by connecting the dots between the things we do and investing in good mental health, for example 'To be honest I just really needed to switch off for a while so I didn't do much, it was great for resetting and investing in my mental health'.

Do you see how you can bring mental health education into your daily life, not just at a formal event or initiative?

A mentally healthy culture requires people to take individual responsibility for their success, including investing in their own mental health and saying no to things that will inhibit sustainable success such as working ridiculously long hours and sacrificing their social life (it may lead to short-term success but will inevitably lead to burnout in the long run). But it also takes organizational responsibility! This means benefits and resources are great, but only while also focusing on policies and working practice that are conducive to long-term success for the individual as well as the business.

A word for HR departments and people professionals

You are amazing! You work tirelessly every day to put out fires, support new hires and make sure people are kept at the forefront of the business, sometimes at the expense of your own health! I've talked to countless HR professionals who are simply leaving their jobs, hoping to find a culture where all their effort will be appreciated and can be more than just a tick-box or fire-fighting exercise but a genuine drive for creating change!

One HR professional told me, 'I did so much for everyone else but when I got burnt out, nobody was there for me and I had to leave'.

This is horrific!

I think sometimes we forget that HR and caring professionals are allowed to get help too! You're allowed to have boundaries, say no, empower people to run with things themselves and get the help of your helpline, a coach, therapist, or digital detox holiday yourself! You're allowed to be a helper and want a life outside of work, you're allowed to not have all the answers, you're allowed to want a strategic approach to mental health but be overwhelmed by events and the little things that make that approach always a little out of reach.

You need allies and leaders to help bring all the big ideas to life!

We need a culture change plan that will ensure environments help people thrive and excel; this will enable focus and productivity and talent retention – besides it just being the right thing to do!

As discussed in the last chapter, focus is going to be the greatest commodity of the next decade.

In a world of distraction, the problem to solve is 'how can we help create the environments to enhance focus to enable creativity and innovation?'

We are fighting against the tide, as social media and technology companies have monetized our attention (through advertising revenue and harvesting personal data) and so they deploy every weapon in their arsenal to keep us distracted. These platforms are set up to make us watch for one more minute or click one more thing as they fight ruthlessly for our attention.

We can mitigate this trend by taking agency over our attention and influences. How often do you really need to see the news? How often do you get stuck in a social media vortex that leaves you feeling empty?

Ways to reset include:

- Having a digital detox of some kind. This could be not watching the news for a while if it makes you anxious, deleting your social apps or having no-meeting days at work. Whatever it looks like for you, it can take us a little while to feel withdrawals from technology and reset into a calmer nervous system.
- Scheduling healthy things into your diary, as your free time will fill up and you'll be less likely to follow old patterns. Trying a new gym class, doing something creative like art or music, connecting with new people, etc will all help reset the balance.

But of course this means prioritizing time for you.

People are often complaining about the lack of free time but really we have the same amount of time we've always had, and more technology to help us automate and speed up our daily tasks than ever before. But societal and cultural pressures to keep busy cause our focus and energy levels to be all over the place, which means that we'll never get to where we want to go and if we do, it's never enough. So we can't just put on another well-being or inclusion webinar or workshop if we're going to change culture. We need to look at our working practices, psychological safety, autonomy and trust for people to manage their time, focus and energy effectively.

And it begins with you.

It doesn't matter if people are remote or not. Everyone is different. Some people have absolutely thrived in a home-working environment and other people have crumbled. People focus better in different places so it's more about offering the education and autonomy to actually do something that maximizes focus and energy – this will enable us to evolve our workplaces for the future while keeping our talent!

So when thinking of your mental health or well-being plan at work, think about the environment that you need in order to support the most energy and focus – it probably involves space for reflection and recovery, and it definitely involves the internal activists who want to help bring your well-being strategy to life.

A summary for activists

- Your behaviours on a daily basis make the biggest difference over time.
- It takes organizational responsibility and personal agency to make real and lasting change at work.
- Be the bridge that connects daily life to mental health education.
- And finally, practise bravery.

Practising the skill of bravery means working on your own thoughts and internal strength, expanding the potential of your brain and saying things that will disrupt the conversation. It's taking risks in telling your story and risks in listening fully to others. It's being brave enough to say 'no' and show up to the world as human, with struggles as well as the ability to thrive.

Bravery doesn't feel brave, it feels like action.

CHAPTER EIGHT

Practical tactics and strategies

You might be thinking to yourself: 'it's all well and good for me to think for myself but WHAT DO I DO?!' We all like a plan and some clean takeaways so my aim in this chapter is to give you exactly what you're after. These tactics can help you press the pause button and actually apply the learning on thinking for yourself, not only to reduce the risk of burnout and depression but to bring happiness, fulfilment and joy to your life.

Thinking for yourself and knowing that you're doing the right thing can be tremendously difficult. When trying to make a decision, have you ever listed all of the advice you've received, evaluated all of your ideas, weighed up the pros and cons, but ended up still feeling just as stuck as when you started? Fundamentally this approach isn't that useful, because it's assuming that there are clear pros and cons or rights and wrongs in the situation, when the reality is life is mostly the grey area in-between. None of the options are objectively wrong, they're just different from one another.

The question is: what do you *want* to do? What feels right for *you*? While you won't know all the variables or consequences of any choice beforehand, you can still take personal responsibility for your life, which of course includes the learning that will come from that choice. That's often why we unconsciously give our agency away – if it doesn't work out then we've always got someone else to blame. We're scared of real autonomy and the responsibility that comes with it.

Thinking for yourself is a practice, so here are a few principles to consider to help prime your autonomy, especially when it comes to investing in yourself and your well-being, which will enable long-term success (whatever that means to you):

Create space

Now before you say you don't have time, let me remind you again of the alternative. Do you have two full years to recover from burnout? Do you have time to fall apart and crash out? If the answer is no then it would serve you well to invest in creating some space now. As Marcus 'Elevation' Taylor (Motiversity, 2022) says, 'Choose your Hard! You can choose the hard of waking up, working out, practising bravery and showing up or you can choose the hard of spiralling into despair or repairing the damage done.'

So create space for thinking! This could be really simple things, like:

- Walking with no headphones on your way to work or during a break (radical I know!)
- Daydreaming (literally staring into nothingness – it's a thing we used to be quite good at!)
- Anything that moves your body to get you connected to your source – dance, tai chi, cartwheels, swimming – nothing too hardcore needed

You don't need to schedule massively long routines for these habits to be worthwhile, you can integrate them into your day. Notice your body sensations, not just your thoughts, and you'll have to sift through your thoughts to decide which ones you want to lean into and which ones you let pass by, as many of them will be influenced by your past patterns and conditioning. On the other hand, your body takes practice to listen to but it is pure wisdom!

Manage information overload

Rather than do more, why not do less? Turn off notifications, take a timed break from a social media platform, don't watch the news, or watch it once a week, pause a newspaper subscription and even have a break from reading personal development books (this can be your last one for a while!).

You've heard the idea of digital detoxes or perhaps switched something off yourself – or like many people you've acted like a true addict and said something like 'I'm not an addict. I can stop any time I want. I just don't want to stop'. Classic! Why not test the theory? When I'm in tech-addiction mode I have to physically put my phone in another room so that I'm not tempted to touch it and after 10 minutes (I'm lying, it takes about three minutes) my thumb starts twitching as if it's missing an appendage. We all have reasons for why we need to be always on:

- I've got to work
- I want to stay connected to friends
- I need to know what's happening in the news
- What if there's an emergency?

These are all perfectly valid reasons we surround ourselves with in order not to see the situation for what it is.

I'm not saying you need to go full monk and live on a mountain for six months with no Wi-Fi and a strict meditation habit to learn to think for yourself. I'm saying get conscious about the information overload that is at you all the time and perhaps what that noise is numbing or helping you avoid. I know we don't do this consciously but we do it nonetheless!

This morning I lay in a blissful massage chair at my new gym. It wasn't busy so I had the room to myself and as the chair tipped me back, I simply closed my eyes, no headphones, no noise, silence. I indulgently lay there for about 15 minutes, I got up and felt tears in my eyes. I'd stopped long enough to feel.

So just experiment for a few days, a week or maybe a month if you can build it up. For me, I don't have any news apps and the notifications on my phone are limited. Every notification ping from your phone triggers a sort of fight-or-flight response in our bodies – we're driven to have a quick check to see whether it's good or bad news. Imagine what that's doing to your nervous system if you have notifications pinging hundreds of times a day!

Experiment and notice what happens in your body – the higher your withdrawals the more you probably need to experiment a little longer!

Critically assess

To critically assess is to question your own biases, influences and judgements, to truly listen to new information before jumping to a conclusion and to make a decision based on what you discover.

It's important to be able to ask yourself internal questions so you can learn how to listen to your own body and thoughts. Now this is different from overthinking and obsessing about what to do, which can become part of the problem – keeping us in a loop of anxiety that can lead to apathy and decision freeze. Progress is not made with a perfect plan, it is made through listening to what you truly want and taking action. This action enables us to iterate along the way.

Asking ourselves reflective questions is also different from paranoia and trusting no one due to some past hurt playing a part in your life now. It's asking yourself a few questions and seeing how you feel, that's all. But again, this takes practice if you've never listened to yourself before and that's OK! Ask yourself things like: I wonder where that idea came from, do I want to buy into it or not – what else might be true in this situation? Who do I know from my past who might answer the same way? How does it make my body feel? What else might be going on here? How does my energy feel? Do I feel tingling excitement or a knot in my belly?

When it comes to our mental health, being able to critically assess includes:

- Ask for a second opinion on professional advice
- Do your research so that your decisions are informed
- Listen to people from varied backgrounds on the topic and identify the aspects that you have agency over – such as lifestyle, environment, health, etc
- Watch or listen to what other people do to discipline their minds and bodies, how they nurture their bodies and souls, what their routines are and other well-being tools that work for them
- Take the pressure off! You don't have to do all of these things at once and different tools will help you at different times

As James Clear outlines in his book *Atomic Habits* (2018), '1% better every day = 37% progress every year!'

Small steps that are aligned to what your body and mind need are much more powerful than 50 steps that everyone else has told you to take.

Hold your opinions loosely

As an evolving being in an evolving world you can only hold so much information, knowledge and thought in your mind. Anything you weigh up now may change in the future based on new variables you simply couldn't have accounted for yet. You may feel certain right now that you'll always think a certain way about something, but the reality is you don't know what you don't know and you don't know how the world around you will develop or what knowledge you'll acquire that you simply didn't have before.

My advice here is to hold your opinions and ideas loosely. By all means, learn like you didn't go to school – nurture curiosity, experience new things, have conversations with people outside your normal circles, engage with the world in a way only you can – and try things on for size, but be open to a new idea challenging your old one.

Rather than going about your day looking for an argument or a way to reinforce your own belief system, instead stay open to new information that can add to what you know or maybe even challenge it completely. Our online world is set up as an echo chamber to reinforce our likes and the belief systems we already hold, as this enables advertisers to hone in their marketing capability to a certain type of person. To them, you are a dataset and unless you consciously find ways to widen your circles you can easily become a version of yourself that is fixed, thereby not growing in neuroplasticity that gives you hope for more happiness and health.

I've learnt that anything I now know is just that, something that feels true to me now but can change over time. Knowing this helps me take risks because I can reassure myself when making a decision that given the variables I know now, I am moving on this path but that's free to change:

> Do the best you can until you know better. Then when you know better, do better. (Attributed to Maya Angelou.)

It's important to nurture playful curiosity – what the psychologist Dr Carol Dweck (2017) calls a growth mindset: 'In a growth mindset, **people believe that their most basic abilities can be developed through dedication and hard work – brains and talent are just the starting point**. This view creates a love of learning and a resilience that is essential for great accomplishment.'

Just because you've had a deep epiphany in a certain setting doesn't mean this now has to be your truth forever. I say this because there are lots of communities, retreats and events that can give you a feeling of love, community and spirituality, which can max out those endorphins and be amazing, and by all means have as many of these experiences as possible. The trouble comes when that one experience becomes our evangelism ground zero and we now think everyone must try to have that one experience as it will very possibly *change their life* too.

The thing is, you had that experience because of all the events that led you to that moment of letting go, connecting or opening up or whatever it was for you. And this can be a wonderful piece of your well-being puzzle to lead you and help you on the path to your version of success. When you hold on tightly to whatever happened and incorporate it into your one truth, your brain gets fixed and begins to block off other truths that the world can continue to enlighten you with.

So hold your ideas as magic but hold them loosely. You cannot hold sky – it is all around you but to hold it tightly in your hands would be ridiculous. It's the same with ideas and experiences, let them flow through you, evolving who you are and opening you up to the vastness of the universe.

Take responsibility for your life

Finally, take responsibility for your life.

I don't mean relentlessly achieve your goals no matter what the cost to your health or practise 20 well-being tools before 7 am. What I mean is, question what your goals are to begin with, assess how your environment is impacting your health, look at your depression, anxiety or burnout with fresh eyes, ask yourself what is influencing your path and then take responsibility for deciding what is right for you.

Sometimes asking yourself what you want and what success really means to you can lead to realizations that mean change needs to happen. This can feel hard and overwhelming!

When I quit my good job to go my own path and then got offered another big job and said no because I knew it would be toxic, I felt that *excited-sick* feeling again, like 'oh my god what am I doing?' but it was my body knowing what my path was, nobody else's, just mine.

I feel it when writing this book. Books have been my gateway into other worlds, a privilege of learning that I can hardly describe. But I'm saying more than I ever have and I feel *excited-sick* at the prospect. What will people think, have I told too much of my story, can I really do this, what will the fallout be? But I know this feeling, I know it well and it has led me to my own voice and living the life that I want. It's not a perfect life, but it's *my* life, it holds power in it because it is mine. Some of you will get the gravity of that statement, some of you will not. It's when you see how your thinking has been hijacked and then fight for decades for an original thought and then act on those thoughts, leading you to a totally different world that you didn't think was possible for someone like you – that's taking responsibility for your life.

Taking responsibility can look like tiny things. Going for a walk, calling a friend, getting support, but it's not all about needing to slow down – these small things are what build bravery and agency over your life and allow you to do the big things you've always dreamed of. If you're ambitious like me and want big, huge things these methods can support you to sustain success long term, and not just for the destination but so you can enjoy the journey along the way. Responsibility is discipline, it's working out when you feel like sleeping, it's having a difficult conversation because it will support progress, it's admitting you don't know something and then learning from that experience, it's playing a part in changing your culture when it's easier to complain about it, it's going for your dreams – but making sure they are yours!

Conclusion

I hope you have taken something away from this book.
I hope you realize that focusing on your well-being and mental health doesn't mean taking a slower path or a less ambitious path, it means instead that you start with questioning your view of success and sustaining the path you want longer term.

It's recognizing that to neglect your well-being in this fast-paced world is to wait until a crisis hits and forces you to stop and reassess your approach to life anyway. So many people are looking for cures to their signs and symptoms through doctors, therapists and allies, but have forgotten how to listen to what their body and mind is telling them! There are some answers that can only come from you.

What is the life you want to build? What's the meaning you want to create for yourself? What matters to you? And crucially, who does your thinking for you?

Do I still give my thoughts away to the highest bidder? Sometimes.

In a world of distraction and influence this isn't just a one-time lesson, it's a practice (just like anything), a skill that we can develop over time.

Managing our mental health is a skill too, just as investing in ourselves is a skill. When we realize it's a skill we realize that we have agency and can practise new ways of being, we can ask ourselves the questions about what we really think. When we do this, a whole world of healthy success opens up to us – but knowing what you want is only the first step.

It's the next steps where the real work begins.

It takes bravery to follow through on your original thought – to live your life differently and challenge the ideas that are thrown at you every day. It takes bravery to invest in yourself, to have boundaries, to question your environment and play a part in changing your culture. Not like an evangelist bombarding your thinking onto everyone else, but like a personal example of what living a good life actually means.

My greatest joy now is my two children – they're young adults now and I look at them with total privilege that they are in my life. That we share ideas, books and experiences. That I am a trusted person in their lives who has taught them, through my own struggle, to think for themselves. These kids rightfully could have been taken from me when they were younger, our whole lives could have gone down a very different path and yet, we made a different version of life. They know the struggle and have learnt from it and while yes, we talk about generational trauma and the impact of my behaviour and past on their psyche, I am not stuck in guilt and repair cycles. I know that in order to help them along their path the best thing I can do is live a good life, to take responsibility for my life and give them space to think for themselves. When we know better we do better.

That's all we can ever do. In our teams and workplaces – as we inspire others with a vision for the future of work, we can lead by example first of all. We can be explicit when we do things to invest in our well-being, we can show through our behaviours that there's another way to live and we can create space for others to truly think for themselves. What does this look like in teams? It looks like slowing down and creating space for thinking but more than that, it means slowing down enough to actually feel. This is a radical concept and not a word I readily use when I do work in corporate settings. I translate the word feel into words like impact and investment – but really, the crucial practice when it comes to success in a new world is checking in on how you feel.

This doesn't mean every feeling or thought is reason to follow it. I *feel* tired, let me not go outside. I *feel* scared, let me not take action. Instead, it's getting to understand your feelings and the wisdom of your body – is your feeling just trying to keep you safe because that's what it's practised in doing, or is it giving you an indication of an injustice or a different way that you need to live?

When you know your body well enough you'll find your own *excited-sick* feeling, the one that's scared but is pushing you out of your zone of comfort, the one that is out of practice but wants to do something brave, the one that is tired but wants to live a radically different life, the one that is unwell but still wants to be honest and take responsibility.

Whatever that feeling is to you. Listen.

Sometimes when you listen you'll know that you need to do something radically different.

I had to leave a toxic cult environment, I had to leave a marriage, I had to leave a job – you may need to radically change things too.

You might be near burnout or in crisis and need to find your balance before making any big changes, that's OK, small steps are the building blocks to great things. What's important is that you begin with you and start taking responsibility for your mental health.

I know there is plenty of uncertainty and fear around us, but I see plenty of hope too!

I see opportunity (finally!) to properly evolve our workplaces into places that are good for our mental health!

I see a mental health narrative that is building traction with an opportunity for each and every one of us who's struggled, who's experienced toxic workplaces, who've been impacted by loss and pain, no matter what our story – to impact our world for the better.

I want us to evolve even further from knowing it's OK not to be OK to it being OK to just be honest – to be amazing, to be tired, to be chilled, ambitious, experiencing depression, anxiety – to bring our emotional world into our work world. To normalize our well-being to the point that it's not just a crisis to solve but is an opportunity for a different future.

Get started today – close this book and go, do one brave act!

References

Introduction

Brown, B (2019) *Braving the Wilderness*, Random House, London

Clark, D (2022) Number of people living alone in the UK from1996 to 2021, Statista, 27 July, www.statista.com/statistics/281616/people-living-alone-uk-by-gender/ (archived at https://perma.cc/W2CJ-5M96)

Hari, J (2019) *Lost Connections*, Bloomsbury Publishing, London

Kline, N (2002) *Time to Think*, Cassell, London

United States Census Bureau (2021) Census Bureau releases new estimates on America's families and living arrangements, 29 November, www.census.gov/newsroom/press-releases/2021/families-and-living-arrangements.html (archived at https://perma.cc/5NKY-6X34)

Chapter 1: Why me?

Aked, J et al (2008) *Five ways to well-being*, Centre for Well-being/New Economics Foundation, https://neweconomics.org/uploads/files/five-ways-to-wellbeing-1.pdf (archived at https://perma.cc/M6UJ-9BHG)

Alcoholics Anonymous (1921) The Just for Today Card

Gawdat, M (2019) *Solve for happy: Engineer your path to joy*, Bluebird, London

Chapter 2: Why you?

Cambridge Dictionary (nd) success (definition), https://dictionary.
cambridge.org/dictionary/english/success (archived at https://
perma.cc/422A-U7XC)

Chopra, D and Tanzi, R E (2013) *Super Brain: Unleashing the
explosive power of your mind*, Rider

Delphis (2020) The mental health continuum is a better model for
mental health, 30 June, https://delphis.org.uk/mental-health/
continuum-mental-health/ (archived at https://perma.cc/
Y3G7-EZEQ)

Edmondson, A (1999) Psychological safety and learning behavior
in work teams, *Administrative Science Quarterly*, 44 (2),
350–83, https://doi.org/10.2307/2666999 (archived at https://
perma.cc/DXX9-VCX5)

Frankl, V (1946/2004) *Man's Search for Meaning: The classic
tribute to hope from the Holocaust*, Rider

REBA (2022) Financial return on EAPs 2022: The pandemic effect,
31 January, https://reba.global/resource/financial-return-on-
eaps-2022-the-pandemic-effect.html# (archived at https://perma.
cc/25C6-NB53)

Seligman, M (2006) *Learned Optimism: How to change your mind
and your life*, Vintage Books USA

World Health Organization/Pan American Health Organization
(2014) *Plan of Action on Mental Health 2015–2020*, https://
www.paho.org/hq/dmdocuments/2015/plan-of-action-on-MH-
2014.pdf (archived at https://perma.cc/R2SG-T2NJ)

Young, K (nd) The science of gratitude – how it changes people,
relationships (and brains!) and how to make it work for you,
Hey Sigmund, www.heysigmund.com/the-science-of-gratitude/
(archived at https://perma.cc/2NPH-5NXU)

Chapter 3: Learning to think for ourselves

Achor, S (2011) *The Happiness Advantage: The seven principles of positive psychology that fuel success and performance at work*, Virgin Books

Aked, A et al (2008) *Five ways to well-being*, Centre for Well-being/ New Economics Foundation, https://neweconomics.org/uploads/ files/five-ways-to-wellbeing-1.pdf (archived at https://perma.cc/ UUN7-ZX6U)

Allen, P (2020) Mental health for all: investing in well-being reaps rewards, LifeWorks, 11 May, https://well-being.lifeworks.com/ uk/resource/mental-health-for-all-investing-in-well-being-reaps-rewards/# (archived at https://perma.cc/4EBJ-XZZL)

Aubrey Marcus Podcast (2022) Episode 354 with Emily Fletcher, 23 March.

Dispenza, J (2012) *Breaking the Habit of Being Yourself: How to lose your mind and create a new one*, Hay House UK, London

McDougall, J (1985) *Theaters of the Mind: Illusion and truth on the psychoanalytic stage*, Routledge, New York

McLean Hospital (2022) The social dilemma: social media and your mental health, 21 January, www.mcleanhospital.org/ essential/it-or-not-social-medias-affecting-your-mental-health (archived at https://perma.cc/NG36-9LG3)

Pick, D (2022) *Brainwashed: A new history of thought control*, Wellcome Collection, London

Oxford Reference (nd) brainwashing (definition), https://www. oxfordreference.com/view/10.1093/oi/authority. 20110803095524780# (archived at https://perma.cc/Z23G-DMH5)

Whyte Jr, W H (1952) Groupthink, *Fortune*, https://fortune. com/2012/07/22/groupthink-fortune-1952/ (archived at https:// perma.cc/7ED3-HHVQ)

World Health Organization (2021) Depression, 13 September, www.who.int/news-room/fact-sheets/detail/depression (archived at https://perma.cc/CJ3C-6NYY)

Chapter 4: Stress, burnout and mental illness

Allen, S (2018) The science of gratitude, white paper, Greater Good Science Center, May, https://ggsc.berkeley.edu/images/uploads/GGSC-JTF_White_Paper-Gratitude-FINAL.pdf (archived at https://perma.cc/RFS7-KNLU)

BetterHelp (2022) Types of anxiety disorders and how you can treat them, 24 August, www.betterhelp.com/advice/anxiety/types-of-anxiety-disorders-and-how-you-can-treat-them/ (archived at https://perma.cc/B8R9-BFEV)

Campbell, L (2021)Why personal boundaries are important and how to set them, PsychCentral, 7 June, https://psychcentral.com/lib/what-are-personal-boundaries-how-do-i-get-some#what-they-are (archived at https://perma.cc/5APP-YLUR)

Cleveland Clinic (2021) Empathy fatigue: how stress and trauma can take a toll on you, 25 June, https://health.clevelandclinic.org/empathy-fatigue-how-stress-and-trauma-can-take-a-toll-on-you/ (archived at https://perma.cc/NFT6-NUSR)

Dispenza, J (2009) *Evolve your Brain: The science of changing your mind*, Health Communications, Inc, Deerfield Beach, FL

Hari, J (2019) *Lost Connections*, Bloomsbury Publishing, London

Leaf, C (2021) *Cleaning Up Your Mental Mess: 5 simple, scientifically proven steps to reduce anxiety, stress and toxic thinking*, Baker Books, Grand Rapids, MI

Merriam-Webster (nd) stigma (definition), https://www.merriam-webster.com/dictionary/stigma (archived at https://perma.cc/2MUY-VG4M)

Nagoski, A and Nagoski, E (2020) *Burnout: Solving your stress cycle*, Vermilion, London

Puleo, G (nd) The biggest challenge in burnout recovery, A new way to work, https://a-new-way-to-work.com/2022/10/03/the-biggest-challenge-in-burnout-recovery/ (archived at https://perma.cc/E7MP-FQ38)

Stanley, E (2021) *Widen the Window: Training your brain and body to thrive during stress and recover from trauma*, Yellow Kite, London

World Health Organization (2019) Burn-out an 'occupational phenomenon': International Classification of Diseases, 28 May, www.who.int/news/item/28-05-2019-burn-out-an-occupational-phenomenon-international-classification-of-diseases (archived at https://perma.cc/7FFR-6JCF)

Chapter 5: Maintenance, attitude and living a good life now

Aked, J et al (2008) *Five ways to well-being*, Centre for Well-being/New Economics Foundation, https://neweconomics.org/uploads/files/five-ways-to-wellbeing-1.pdf (archived at https://perma.cc/694H-YFSQ)

Brown, B (2022) *The Gifts of Imperfection*, Hazelden Publishing, Center City, MN

Kemp, S (2022) Digital 2022: Time spent using connected tech continues to rise, DataReportal, 26 January, https://datareportal.com/reports/digital-2022-time-spent-with-connected-tech (archived at https://perma.cc/88V3-ZYHR)

Nagoski, A and Nagoski, E (2020) *Burnout: Solving your stress cycle*, Vermilion, London

Chapter 6: Supporting others

Kline, N (2002) *Time to Think*, Cassell, London
TED (2010) The power of vulnerability, Brené Brown (online
video) https://www.youtube.com/watch?v=iCvmsMzlF7o
(archived at https://perma.cc/QE59-E7YJ)

Chapter 7: Internal activism and changing the world of work

TED (2012) The happy secret to better work, Shawn Achor,
1 February (online video) https://www.youtube.com/watch?v=
fLJsdqxnZb0 (archived at https://perma.cc/84YD-QZWD)

Chapter 8: Practical tactics and strategies

Clear, J (2018) *Atomic Habits*, Random House Business Books,
London
Dweck, C (2017) *Mindset: Changing the way you think to fulfil
your potential*, Robinson
Motiversity (2022) Choose your hard, 14 June (online video)
https://www.youtube.com/watch?v=heQ18p8zu74 (archived at
https://perma.cc/C2AY-M3RL)

Acknowledgements

There are of course a million people and influences that have made me who I am today and helped in the process of writing this book. Even the things that may have seemed negative have shaped and given me what I need. So, with that in mind, here are a few acknowledgements to name.

My first library card at the age of 13, which opened up a world of books and learning for me.

My strange childhood, for giving me a window into the world of people and cultures.

My beautiful kids who are now young adults. They teach me every day to show up to life and, once upon a time, played a part in saving my life.

To my ex-husband and his family, for standing by me through the addiction years and doing everything in their power to support me as a person – I am forever grateful.

To all the authors who came before me, who showed me the power of words.

To my parents and the cult – the story wasn't all bad and the good times shaped me, too.

To my partner, David, for teaching me how to love, for making me feel safe and for picking up the pieces when it all feels too hard.

To my big sister, Phebe, who was a first reader of my story; who called me crying saying that I'd given words to something that so many of our generation have no words for. I cried back, because she's the person who knows all of the story and knows what it took to get here. She's also the wisest person I know.

To everyone who's made it through something excruciating or traumatic, from my generation of cult kids to those of you who've messaged me or spoken to me about the losses you've faced, the traumas you've been through, and the mental health struggles you manage. When we share our stories, we see what's possible, we move from the shadows into the light and together we change the narrative. I see you, I'm proud of you, let's keep moving to better things – together.

And, of course, to Matt James from Kogan Page, who believed in what I had to say and guided me in a way that felt safe, empathetic and important – thank you.

INDEX

Page locators in italics denote information within a figure.